What the experts are saying about
Ultimate Fitness through Martial Arts

"An excellent addition to any martial artist's library . . . a definite 'A'. "
- Action Martial Arts Magazine

"The many photos and tips will delight those already involved in the martial arts." *- The Bookwatch*

"A serious self-help book." *- Eclectic Book Reviews*

"*Ultimate Fitness* is a must for anyone who wants to increase their fitness level by pursuing martial arts training. Well written, thorough. "
- Northwest Warrior News

"The most thorough and informative book on martial arts conditioning, fitness and exercise available." *- Business Master Trade Journal*

"A one-stop reference for martial artists and fitness enthusiasts."
- Taekwondo Times Magazine

"Designed to be read on a day to day basis . . . if you read *Ultimate Fitness* you can become truly fit." *- Friend's Review*

"As the popularity of *Ultimate Fitness* suggests, physical fitness is among the most compelling attractions of martial arts training."
- Sky Magazine

"Master Sang H. Kim is one of the most active and insightful taekwondo instructors in the world today."
- WTF Taekwondo Magazine

"Master Kim has seen martial arts from both sides and knows what works . . . A three dimensional master." *- Combat Magazine*

ULTIMATE
FITNESS
Through Martial Arts

by
Sang H. Kim

Turtle Press   Hartford

ULTIMATE FITNESS THROUGH MARTIAL ARTS

Photographs by Marc Yves Regis
Cover Design by John Oldham Studios

To contact the author or to order additional copies of this book:

Turtle Press
401 Silas Deane Hwy.
P.O. Box 290206
Wethersfield, CT 06129-0206

Library of Congress Card Catalog Number 93-13327

ISBN 1-880336-02-2
ISBN 978-1-880336-02-1

First Edition

Library of Congress Cataloguing-in-Publication Data

Kim, Sang H.
      Ultimate fitness through martial arts / by Sang H. Kim. - - 1st ed.
            p.   cm.
      Includes index
      ISBN 1-880336-02-2 : $16.95
      ISBN 978-1-880336-02-1 : $16.95
      1. Martial arts - - Training.   2. Physical fitness.   I Title.
GV1102.7.T7K56   1993
      796.8 - - dc20   93-13327

NOTE TO READERS

Throughout this book "he" is used to refer to people. This is for ease of reading only and should be taken to mean he or she where appropriate.

BEFORE YOU BEGIN

Exercises and activities contained in this book are strenuous and may result in injury to the practitioner. As with all exercise programs, consult a physician before beginning.

Contents

CHAPTER 1: THE QUEST
WHAT IS FITNESS? 10
MAINTAINING FITNESS 11
EXERCISE METHODOLOGY 11
WARM-UPS 13
HOW TO USE THIS BOOK 15
YOUR PERSONALIZED WORKOUT 18

CHAPTER 2: POWER 21
WHAT IS IT? 21
HOW TO IMPROVE 24

CHAPTER 3: SPEED 55
WHAT IS IT? 55
HOW TO IMPROVE 57

CHAPTER 4: PERCEPTION 75
WHAT IS IT? 75
HOW TO IMPROVE 77

CHAPTER 5: COORDINATION 91
WHAT IS IT? 91
HOW TO IMPROVE 93

CHAPTER 6: BALANCE 107
WHAT IS IT? 107
HOW TO IMPROVE 111

CHAPTER 7: AGILITY 131
WHAT IS IT? 131
HOW TO IMPROVE 132

CHAPTER 8: FLEXIBILITY 147
WHAT IS IT? 147
HOW TO IMPROVE 148

CHAPTER 9: ENDURANCE 193
    WHAT IS IT? 193
    HOW TO IMPROVE 195

CHAPTER 10: ACCURACY 205
    WHAT IS IT? 205
    HOW TO IMPROVE 207

CHAPTER11: TIMING 217
    WHAT IS IT? 217
    HOW TO IMPROVE 218

CHAPTER 12: MENTAL STRENGTH 227
    WHAT IS IT? 227
    HOW TO IMPROVE 229

NUTRITIO N 235
    THE COMPONENTS OF GOOD NUTRITION 236
    NUTRITIONAL CONCERNS OF ATHLETES 239

INJURY PREVENTIO N 241
    SAFETY IN THE TRAINING AREA 242
    BEFORE YOU BEGIN 242
    DURING YOUR WORKOUT 243
    WORKING WITH A PARTNER 244
    STAYING FIT 244
    OVERUSE INJURIES 245

SAMPLE WO RKO UTS 247
    DESIGNING YOUR PERSONALIZED WORKOUT 248
    USING THE SAMPLE PLANS 249

1

THE QUEST

The quest for the ultimate physical condition is as old as man himself. In the early years, it was a matter of survival. Man against man, man against beast. The fit survived and the weak perished. Without modern transportation, agriculture, weaponry, communications equipment, construction methods and food distribution, early man had to rely on himself or his kin for almost every aspect of life. The physical demands of life were extreme and fitness was a necessity not a luxury or goal.

Time passed and innovations made life easier with every passing decade. Now, walking from the car to the mall is considered by some to be exercise. Imagine what our ancestors might think of us now. While we live several times longer than they did, they were probably much more in tune with their bodies than we are. Our lives are prolonged by advanced medicine, balanced diets and carefully planned exercise - exercise that makes up for the natural workout our bodies would get, if not for the conveniences of modern man.

So our quest for the ultimate physical condition is not so much for daily survival as it is for our long term physical, emotional, spiritual and mental health. We workout to feel better and live longer, to compete and win, to look good and feel good.

As martial artists, we also work hard at fitness to help us perform better in our artistic and sporting pursuits. Without basic physical fitness, participation in a demanding physical pursuit is prohibitive. Once basic fitness is achieved, we can begin our pursuit of peak fitness - the condition that will allow us to excel in our art and reach our full potential.

WHAT IS FITNESS?

Performance fitness is defined in physical education terms as those qualities that provide the individual with the ability to successfully participate in sporting activities. The fundamental components of skill related fitness are speed, agility, coordination, power and balance. In addition to that definition of general fitness, martial artists must add the qualities of flexibility, accuracy, perception, timing, endurance and mental conditioning.

Development of these eleven attributes characterizes a balanced training plan for martial artists of all styles. When you are in good physical condition, learning new skills is easier. If you have to learn and get in shape at the same time, you are working twice as hard as the fit athlete.

BENEFITS OF FITNESS

There are many benefits of being in good physical condition. The most commonly experienced improvements are:

1. improved efficiency in sport performance
2. circulatory efficiency and decrease in circulatory problems
3. stress reduction
4. weight management
5. better sleep and digestion
6. increased confidence
7. higher level of energy for daily tasks
8. decreased risk of injury
9. joy of participating in the activity itself
10. feeling of being in control of your life
11. self-discipline

These benefits increase as you progress in skill level. Most important, though, is the feeling of a renewed sense of energy and enjoyment in your life.

MAINTAINING FITNESS

In addition to regular exercise, there are a number of life-style changes you may need to make to maintain your overall desired level of fitness.

1. don't overtrain
2. exercise year round
3. relax during exercise and in your daily life
4. eat a balanced diet
5. maintain a reasonable weight
6. don't smoke or abuse drugs
7. consume alcohol in moderation (healthy adults only)
8. relieve stress regularly

EXERCISE METHODOLOGY

Exercise has varying degrees of effectiveness.   People training side by side in the same program experience varying degrees of improvement. Do not be distressed if you see your friends progressing ahead of you. Everyone starts at a different level and progresses within their own limitations. Rather than comparing yourself with others, compare your present self with your past self. Are you stronger today than you were last month or six months ago? If you can consistently answer yes to your self tests, you are progressing toward your goals at an acceptable pace.

As you plan your training schedule, keep the following five rules uppermost in your mind.

Specificity

Exercises should be directed to improve the target activity. If your goal is high kicks, focus on lower body agility, strength and flexibility. If your goal is smooth, flowing movements work on flexibility, balance and coordination. Tailor your exercise activities to fit your target activities and work at the same speed and intensity of your goal activity. If you are training for a professional kickboxing match, hit hard, get hit and work on endurance exercises. If you are training for forms competition, do every form with the focus and rhythm you are striving for. If you think you can go easy in practice and then pour it on when you need to, you will be disappointed when reality strikes.

Overload

Overload refers to the increase in intensity, frequency, load and duration of training that is required to produce gains in any area. The best way to achieve consistent gains is by alternating periods of high intensity work with low intensity recovery activities. Through alternation, the body adjusts and recovers regularly, creating change. Consistent periods of high intensity exercise result in stress, fatigue, injury and even diminished skills. Consistent periods of low intensity exercise fail to stress the body enough to create changes.

Overload should not lead to over training. Proper overload training stresses the body enough to challenge it but not so much as to damage or injure it. Similarly, the low intensity recovery period should facilitate growth and rejuvenate minor traumas.

Reversibility

Improvement comes from regular demands that stress the body beyond its previous level of ability. Without regular workouts, deconditioning can occur in as little as two to four weeks after the discontinuation of training. The onset of deconditioning is evidenced by the diminishing of endurance, fine motor coordination and strength. In terms of specific attributes, flexibility and timing decrease most rapidly followed by skill, speed, endurance and strength.

Deconditioning creates the opening for potential injuries. If you have to take off more than a few weeks, restart gradually and at a lower level than when you stopped training. Attempting to restart at your previous level can lead to injuries and a further loss of conditioning. This downward spiral causes many athletes to discontinue their pursuit of fitness or sports participation.

Individuality

Individuals respond differently to the same exercise program. Although the direction of change is the same for everyone (i.e. everyone gets stronger through strength training) the level and speed of improvement varies widely and comes in spurts. Expect plateaus occasionally, usually followed by a sudden spurt of improvement and then eventually another plateau. As long as your progress continues in a general upward motion, you have nothing to be concerned about.

Balance

Everyone has a dominate side, right or left, and dominate skills. For example, you are flexible, your brother is strong and your sister is coordinated. Unfortunately, these strong points can also be your weaknesses. If you think you can never be as a strong as your bother or as coordinated as your sister, you may neglect to develop your weak points. Relying only on your strong points allows you to get by, but rarely to excel. Develop your weaknesses along with your strengths. While your left hand may never be as adept as your right, you can create a usable weapon with some effort.

WARM-UPS

Warm-up before every workout. In general, it is impossible to bring about total flexibility without warming up. Always take the time for a complete warm-up. One of the leading causes of serious injuries is improper or total lack of a warm-up. Your body cannot function dynamically in its normal, cool state.

Spend at least ten to twenty minutes engaging in gross motor activity like jogging, skipping rope, bicycling or aerobics before beginning stretching and vigorous exercise.   An effective warm-up raises the body temperature about two degrees above normal. You know you have achieved your warm-up when you break a light sweat throughout your body.

Effects of the Warm-up

Once you reach this increased body temperature, several favorable events take place to prepare you for strenuous activity.

1. a **decrease in muscle viscosity** (stickiness) allowing your muscles to contract and relax more rapidly over a longer period.
2. an **increase in mechanical efficiency**
3. an **increase in the oxygen supply** to the muscles through increased blood flow.
4. a **decrease in lactic acid**, due to increased blood flow, which improves muscle performance and reduces post exercise stiffness and pain
5. an **increase in flexibility** in tendons and ligaments
6. an **increase in cardiovascular response** and improved cardiovascular capacity allowing for a heavier work load

All of these activities are necessary for safe and effective physical work to take place. The better you warm-up, the better you perform. If you think you don't have time to warm-up, consider the time needed to rehabilitate a torn muscle or ligament.

Types of Warm-ups

There are three types of warm-ups: passive, nonspecific and specific.

1. **Passive warm-ups** are those that raise the body temperature through means other than physical activity like saunas, hot showers or liniments. Except in specialized cases, they are the least effective means of warming up because they raise the body temperature without engaging the joints and muscles in activity.

2. **Nonspecific warm-ups** are those that involve the large muscle groups and are not directly related to the target activity. Examples are moderate levels of swimming, bicycling, jogging and general gross motor movement. They are good to get your body going at the beginning of your workout because they are low demand exercises.

3. **Specific warm-ups** are those that concentrate on the muscle groups to be used in the workout. For example, leg warm-ups for kicking, trunk and arm warm-ups for grappling and upper body warm-ups for striking. Specific warm-ups should follow nonspecific warm-ups. They are the most beneficial type of warm-up because they create muscle efficiency, reduce injuries in frequently used muscles and joints and enhance neuromuscular conditioning.

Toward the end of your nonspecific warm-ups, begin specific flexibility exercises including joint rotations, dynamic stretches and static stretches.

BEFORE YOU BEGIN

Before you begin the exercises in this book or in any program, have a physical exam to determine that you are fit enough to begin exercising without limitation. If your physician places limitations on your exercise program or you are limited by a previous injury, stay within your limits. The goal of exercise is to enhance your body, not to damage it further.

When you are cleared for exercise, remember to always warm-up purposefully and never train when you are ill or injured. Use common sense and listen to your body - it doesn't lie.

HOW TO USE THIS BOOK

The core section of this book is divided into eleven chapters, each encompassing a single physical attribute required for martial arts performance. The chapters begin with a basic definition of the attribute followed by a look at its sources.   Next is an overview of how each characteristic applies specifically to martial arts of various types and then how you can improve it through training.

Some chapters include general cautions to follow for that category of exercise. This introductory material is followed by specific exercises you can use to achieve each attribute. Exercises are arranged in groups for your convenience. Each exercise is broken down as follows:

① Name/Number
The name and number of the exercise used throughout this book.

② i,p,g,e
These symbols indicate what is required for the exercises:

i - can be done by individuals

p - requires a partner

g- can be done in groups, or in some cases requires a group

e - requires equipment or has a variation that requires equipment

③ Correct execution
Describes and illustrates the steps or procedure of the exercise.

④ Variations
Explains exercises that are similar in benefits but have slight changes in execution. Variations are pictured where necessary.

⑤ Main benefit
Describes the primary result of the exercise.

⑥ Also improves
Lists additional benefits. Most exercises have overlapping benefits and are featured only in the chapter that details their main benefit.

⑦ Martial arts applications
Describes the applicability of this exercise to your martial arts training.

⑧ Cautions
Gives warnings of potential injuries or hazards and suggests exercises to avoid if you have a current or previous injury to a specific part of the body.

SAMPLE EXERCISE FORMAT

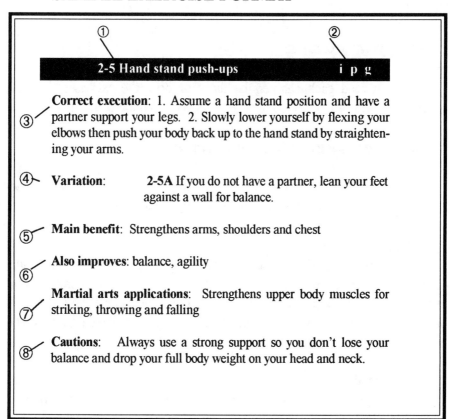

① ②

2-5 Hand stand push-ups i p g

③ **Correct execution**: 1. Assume a hand stand position and have a partner support your legs. 2. Slowly lower yourself by flexing your elbows then push your body back up to the hand stand by straightening your arms.

④ **Variation**: 2-5A If you do not have a partner, lean your feet against a wall for balance.

⑤ **Main benefit**: Strengthens arms, shoulders and chest

⑥ **Also improves**: balance, agility

⑦ **Martial arts applications**: Strengthens upper body muscles for striking, throwing and falling

⑧ **Cautions**: Always use a strong support so you don't lose your balance and drop your full body weight on your head and neck.

YOUR PERSONALIZED WORKOUT

1. Select your exercises

As you read each chapter, highlight or note the exercises that are beneficial to you or that are compatible with your training plan.

2. Organize your exercises into a workout

When you finish the book, consult the sample workouts for a suggested order and number of repetitions for each exercise you select.

Beginners

If you are a beginner, select a variety of exercises for each attribute and combine them into two separate workouts with different themes.   For example, make one upper body workout and one lower body workout or one hard workout and one easy workout. Use them on alternating days for variety and safety.

Advanced

If you are an active martial artist, you need more quantity and variety in your training plans. You can group similar exercises together into single training sessions and train on alternating days. For example, endurance and flexibility on Monday, Wednesday and Friday, and speed and power on Tuesday, Thursday and Saturday. Or, you can integrate exercises from different areas into several separate plans and work some of each, with different exercises, every day. See the sample workout section for more details on these options.

3. Fit your workout into your schedule

Finally, choose which days and at what time to workout, and you have designed a primary workout plan that you can use at home to develop a fit and ready condition for your martial arts training.

SUPPLEMENTARY OR PRIMARY TRAINING

If you are currently training in an organized program, you probably want to use this book to supplement your structured training sessions. When designing a supplemental workout plan, work on attributes like endurance that require more time to develop than is allotted in class and areas where you feel weak. Since your instructor cannot focus on everyone's personal weaknesses in class, spend time on your own to bring yourself up to or beyond the class standard.

Whether you create a supplemental or primary workout plan, use the benchmark tests at the end of each chapter to track your progress and motivate yourself toward consistency. As you improve, your body's needs change. Periodically reread each chapter to select more challenging exercises and reset your fitness goals.

And remember, designing your workout plan is only the first step. Following your plan, analyzing your progress and reaching for your goals are the secret to achieving ultimate fitness.

INSTRUCTOR'S NOTES

Variety is the spice of life and you owe it to your students to spice up their classes. Conditioning should be enjoyable as well as beneficial. After reading this book, look at your current warm-ups, cool downs and conditioning sessions and consider how you can improve them. If you need help in reorganizing, ask yourself the following questions:

1. Am I doing warm-up exercises in the proper order?
2. Am I covering the required attributes in every class?
   Beginners: coordination, balance, flexibility
   Intermediate: agility, power, accuracy, endurance
   Advanced: timing, perception, speed, mental training
3. Am I providing adequate time for conditioning exercise?
4. Have I implemented injury prevention methods?
5. Am I developing all areas of the body equally?
6. Do I place enough emphasis on developing the muscles required for the skills I teach most frequently?
7. Do I regularly rotate or vary warm-up, cool-down and conditioning routines to avoid boredom, overuse injuries and poor exercise habits?
8. Do the conditioning and warm-up exercises I use relate directly to the learning portion of the class?
9. Am I using the correct number of repetitions and sets for the students' ability level?
10. Do assistant instructors understand and follow the proper procedures for warm-ups and exercises?
11. Do I regularly use exercise games, especially for children, to remind students that fitness is fun and rewarding?

Ask yourself these questions regularly. Habits develop quickly and without warning. A prefabricated warm-up and conditioning routine may be comfortable for you, but your students will become bored easily. Student's needs change at every level and these needs must be challenged and fulfilled so further progress can take place. Stay fresh and constantly challenge the structure and content of your exercise routines. Your students will appreciate it and you will constantly have a new outlook on teaching.

2

POWER

WHAT IS IT?

Power is a combination of strength and explosiveness. It is created by releasing maximum muscular force at maximum speed. To increase power, you must increase both speed and strength. By exerting strength with speed, you take advantage of both the force generated by the muscles and the momentum created through the speed.

There are three types of power:

Explosive power - the ability to exert maximum force in one or many dynamic acts. Example: Breaking a board with a kick.

Static power - the maximum force a person can exert for a short period. Example: Bench press.

Dynamic power - the ability to exert muscular force repeatedly or continuously over time. Example: Heavy bag workout.

HOW DOES IT APPLY TO MARTIAL ARTS?

Since martial arts applications are, in their purest form, a conflict between opposing forces, increased power gives you a significant advantage. The ability to strike with power is basic to most martial arts. Similarly, in throwing or grappling arts, power is necessary to control, throw and immobilize the opponent. Though many arts stress finesse over power, the ability to recruit and mobilize muscles quickly is ultimately necessary to react to the opponent and apply a wide range of techniques.

In martial arts, power is magnified in many ways. Some common examples:

1. Move the entire body as one unit.
2. Focus force into one area.
3. Use stable stances for upper body blocking, striking and throwing.
4. Use the lever action of joints.
5. Create reaction force through coupled movements

WHERE DOES IT COME FROM?

Power is derived from muscular ability. The human body contains over 400 muscles that can be broken in two classes: smooth and striated. Smooth muscles are those that perform the involuntary functions of the body including circulation and digestion. Striated muscles are those that can be voluntarily contracted, such as the muscle groups in the arms and legs. These muscles are the source of power.

Slow and fast twitch muscle fibers

Striated muscles are made up of two types of fibers: slow twitch and fast twitch. Slow twitch fibers are designed for activity that must be sustained for a long time like distance running. They have a high capacity for aerobic energy production and can remain active for hours while producing relatively small amounts of lactic acid. This is important because lactic acid build-up in the muscle tissue causes the muscle to fatigue and eventually renders it unable to continue working. Low levels of lactic acid mean more capacity for work. People who have a high percentage of slow twitch fibers excel at endurance activities.

Conversely, people with a greater proportion of fast twitch fibers excel in explosive strength activities. Fast twitch fibers have a high capacity for anaerobic energy production, which allows them to produce intense power and speed of contraction. Such intensive work also causes them to accumulate large amounts of lactic acid and fatigue quickly. (For a more detailed definition of aerobic and anaerobic, see "Chapter 9: Endurance")

Based on this, the answer to developing power seems obvious - increase the percentage of fast twitch muscle fibers in your body. Unfortunately, this is not possible. The ratio of fast and slow twitch muscle fibers is determined early in life and cannot be markedly changed. Studies have shown that distance runners have high percentages of slow twitch fibers and sprinters have high percentages of fast twitch fibers. Yet it has been concluded that the activity itself is not responsible for this phenomenon. Instead, researchers believe that distance runners take up endurance sports because they naturally excel in this area. In the same respect, sprinters are naturally fast and gravitate toward the sport in which they excel.

Although you cannot change the ratio of muscle fibers, you can improve what you have. In the average person, slow and fast twitch muscle fibers are generally intermingled, with a higher percentage of fast twitch fibers present. Through training, you can improve the metabolic efficiency of either type of muscle fiber. Explosive strength training stresses the fast twitch muscle fibers repeatedly, causing them to become stimulated and teaching them to work more efficiently.

Muscle movement

There are two basic ways that force is generated and controlled. The contraction of a muscle is determined by the types of muscle fibers recruited and the firing rate of the neurons within the muscle.

First, let's look at how your body decides which types of muscle fibers to use. The voluntary contraction of a muscle begins with the recruitment of the smallest units of slow twitch muscles. These motor units (muscle fiber groups) have the lowest response threshold, create the least amount of tension and are the most resistant to fatigue. As muscle tension increases, more motor units are recruited from the larger fast twitch fibers. As tension continues to rise, fewer motor units need to be activated because the large fast twitch units contain more plentiful and more powerful muscle fibers. But because these large fibers are the ones that generate peak tension in the muscle, they fatigue quickly and require more recovery time.

As a practical illustration, compare the difference in muscle fatigue you feel when walking and when sprinting. If you walk or sprint, you are using the same basic muscle groups over the same distance. But few people can sprint even half the distance they can walk before their legs simply refuse to go any farther. Walking requires less tension in the muscles and therefore relies on the low threshold, low tension motor units. Sprinting, on the other hand, requires maximum muscle tension for every stride. The muscle fibers' ability to produce maximum tension repeatedly over long periods of time is poor and the legs tire quickly.

Besides the amount and type of muscle fibers recruited, muscle tension and speed of contraction is determined by the rate at which the skeletomotor neurons stimulate the muscle fibers. The more frequently the neurons fire, the more tension that is produced in the muscle. At peak tension, the neuron fires so rapidly that the muscle fiber is unable to relax from one stimulation to the next. The result is the generation of maximum force.

HOW TO IMPROVE

Power consists of both speed and strength. Since speed is a key training component for martial artists, this section focuses on improving strength only. Speed is covered in more depth in the next chapter.

Isometric or Isotonic

Strength is increased by repeatedly stressing the target muscle groups over time. There are three common ways of creating the required stress: isotonic, isometric and isokinetic exercise. Isokinetic exercise requires exercise machines, so this section will examine the more readily available methods of isometric and isotonic exercise.

Normal muscle movement is isotonic. One muscle lengthens while the other contracts in complementary pairs. A good example of isotonic movement is weight training. As you lift the weight and then return it to its original position, your muscles lengthen and contract alternately through the full range of motion.

To understand isometric exercise, imagine you try to lift the same weight and it does not move. No matter how hard you work it remains in the same place. The muscular response you experience when applying force against an immovable object such as this is an isometric contraction. One muscle lengthens and the opposing muscle is prevented from contracting because the stationary weight prevents the muscles from moving through their full range of motion. Building tension in the muscle while preventing it from shortening was once thought to bring dramatic gains in strength. Studies of isometric exercise have since proven it to be an effective, but not miraculous, way of improving strength gradually.

One drawback of isometric exercise is that the muscle is strengthened only in the exact position of the isometric contraction. If you push against the floor with your elbow bent at a ninety degree angle, your arm muscles are strengthened in that position, but you have to repeat the pushing at eighty degrees, seventy degrees and every other position between. Doing simple push-ups, an isotonic exercise, can be much more efficient because you work the entire range of motion, and strengthen the corresponding muscles, in a single action.

Increased strength

The key to effective and consistent strength gains is to apply the proper amount of stress in the correct way at the proper frequency.

Proper amount of stress

Too much stress can easily cause time-loss injuries, injuries that require you to take time off from your exercise program to recover. Taking time off means you have to start over where you left off, or more likely, at a lower level than when you were injured. To prevent overuse and stress injuries, work at your own pace. Don't try to get in shape quickly by doing 200 sit-ups on your first day. Start with a comfortable number of each exercise.

To determine a good number of repetitions, work through as many repetitions as you can until you feel minor discomfort in your muscles. Do a few more repetitions and stop there. Stay with this number until you can complete it without difficulty and then add a few more repetitions. The last ten to twenty percent of the repetitions should always be fairly difficult to complete.

Example: If you can do thirty sit-ups comfortably, set thirty-five as your starting point. After a few sessions, thirty five will become comfortable and you can add more repetitions. As you get into higher repetitions, you may begin to advance more slowly than you did at first. This is normal. Stay at your current number of repetitions as long as you need to.

A gradual increase in work load allows you to reap maximum benefits with minimal injuries.

Correct way of exercising

Execute exercises exactly as you learn them. Cheating on an exercise to squeeze out a few extra repetitions does more harm than good in the long run. Failing to flex your arms fully during push-ups may allow you to do ten more than usual, but it has less effect on your arm strength than push-ups done correctly. If you can do only five push-ups correctly, then do just five. If you stick to the correct form and are consistent, five will turn into ten and ten into twenty and so on.

Each exercise is designed to work specific muscles and produce specific benefits. Make an effort to understand what these benefits are and stick to the correct way of performing each movement.

Proper frequency

For best results, do strengthening exercises two to three times a week. Strength training causes minor tears in your muscle fibers that need about forty-eight hours to heal fully. During this recovery period your muscles become stronger and thicker creating the increases in size and strength that you are training so hard to achieve. When you interrupt the recovery period, you hinder the efforts of your body to produce the results you want.

Guidelines for a workout plan

1. Warm-up

Spend at least ten to fifteen minutes engaging in an aerobic activity that stimulates the large muscle groups of your body. Examples are jogging, biking (road or stationary) and jumping rope. The goal of your warm-up is to break a light sweat and prepare your body for more strenuous work.

2. Load

The load is the amount of weight the muscle bears during the exercise. It can be increased by using weights or by altering the position of your body during the exercises. In weight training, a load of sixty to eighty percent of your maximum liftable weight is enough to produce gains in strength.

3. Sets

Sets are groups of exercises with a brief rest between. If you do 100 push-ups during your workout, break them into four sets of twenty-five each. By resting between sets, you can increase the intensity of each set of exercises.

4. Repetitions

A repetition is the completion of a single exercise. When deciding how many repetitions to include for each exercise, use the guidelines described in the "Proper amount of stress" section.

5. Progression

Progression means increasing the amount of the load as well as the number of sets and repetitions to produce an increased challenge and steady gains in strength. Your workout should always offer you a challenge.

6. Breath control

Breath control is a familiar practice for martial artists and is easily transferred to your conditioning exercises. As in the martial arts, never hold your breath when you are physically exerting yourself. Holding your breath during a strenuous exercise decreases the oxygen supply to your brain which can cause you to pass out.

7. Consistency

Consistency is the hallmark of champions.

CAUTIONS

Before you begin the exercises listed in this section, take note of the following general cautions regarding strength training. Specific cautions follow the individual exercises where applicable.

❖ Strength training should cause some discomfort in your muscles both during and after exercise. If you have any pain in your joints during strengthening exercises, stop immediately. Joint pain during weight bearing exercises is an indication that your muscles are not strong enough to carry the current load. When your muscles cannot bear the weight of an activity, they transfer the overload to the tendons and ligaments of the corresponding joints. Tendons and ligaments are not designed for this type of work and can be strained or torn easily. To ease joint pain during an exercise, try decreasing the weight of the load or increasing the angle of the joint.

Example: If you have pain during squats, increase the angle of the joint by bending your knees only ninety degrees rather than doing a full squat. If you have shoulder pain during push ups, do them while standing and pressing against a wall. By reducing the gravitational pull exerted on your body during prone push-ups, you lessen the weight load on your shoulder joint.

❖ Always use a spotter or partner when working with free weights, weight machines or strengthening devices.

❖ When doing leg strengthening exercises, use caution in bending the knees past ninety degrees (as in squats and lunges) because the potential for knee injury increases significantly when the joint must simultaneously flex and bear weight.

❖ Lift weight properly. If you cannot lift your target weight for at least eight repetitions without cheating, move to a smaller weight.

❖ Remember that your strength decreases in a few weeks when you do not exercise. If you take off more than a few weeks, do not try to start where you left off.

EXERCISES

Strengthening exercises are divided into three categories:

1. Neck, arms and shoulders (# 2-1 to 2-6)
2. Chest, abdomen and back (# 2-7 to 2-11)
3. Buttock and legs (#2-12 to 2-18)

Most of these strengthening exercises can be done without weights or equipment, making them suitable for those who do not have access to a gym or equipment. In some exercises, weights or other equipment can be added to enhance the effectiveness or increase the challenge of the exercise.

2-1 Bridge (front)   i

Correct execution: 1. Kneel down and place your head on the floor in front of you. 2. Gradually lift your knees from the floor, shifting your weight onto your head and the balls of your feet. 3. Gently rotate your head forward and to the right and left. 4. Return slowly to the starting position.

Main benefit: Strengthens the neck and back muscles.

Also improves: coordination, flexibility, agility, balance

Martial arts applications: Strong neck muscles help prevent knockouts that result from blows to the head. Strong neck and back muscles also aid in falling correctly.

1. START: Kneel with your head on the floor

2. Shift weight to your head and feet   3. Rotate

Variation: **2-1A** Rear bridge
1. Lying on your back, bend your knees and raise your hips off the floor.
2. Gradually shift your weight onto your head and feet only. 3. Rotate gently to the right and left. 4. Slowly return to the starting position.

Cautions: This exercise places a high level of stress on the spine and neck. Extreme caution should be observed in all phases of bridging exercises.

1.START: Lie down and raise your hips

2. Shift your weight to your head and feet

2-2 Push-ups   i p g

Correct Execution: Push-ups should be done with the legs straight and the hips and upper body aligned. Bend the elbows to ninety degrees when you lower your body and straighten them fully when you raise it.

Main benefit: Strengthens the upper body, especially the chest, arms and shoulders. See variations for specific areas of benefit.

Martial arts applications: Strengthens striking and throwing skills.

Cautions: Knuckle push-ups should be done by adults only. Push-ups done on the back of the hands strain the wrist and should be done with caution by adults only.

Conventional push-ups (2-2)

Hands beneath shoulders (2-2A)

Hands out to the side (2-2B)

Hands above the head (2-2C)

Variations: **2-2A** Hands placed beneath shoulders (for triceps/arms)
2-2B Hands placed out to the side (for chest/pectorals)
2-2C Hands above the head (for shoulders)
2-2D Push-ups on knuckles (for wrists/fingers)
2-2E Push-ups on the back of the hand (for wrists/forearms)
2-2F Rolling push-ups - Begin with legs in semi-straddle
position. Dip chest forward and pass over hands.
2-2G Have a partner hold your legs off the floor
2-2H With partner, start in push-up position. You do 1 push-
up then he does 1. Then you do 2 and he does 2.
While he is doing push-ups, stay in the start position.
2-2I Do each push-up slowly counting fifteen as you go
down and fifteen as you go back up.

Knuckle push-ups (2-2D)

Back of the hand push-ups (2-2E)

Rolling push-ups (2-2F)

2-3 Fist clench   i g e

Correct execution: Tightly clench and then relax your fist

Variation: **2-3A** Hold a soft object, such as a tennis ball in your hand and clench tightly.

Main benefit: Strengthens grip

Martial arts applications: Improves grip strength for grabbing opponents in close combat applications like throwing and locking techniques and for gripping weapons. Also strengthens the fist for punching and striking.

1. Tightly clench your fist (2-3)

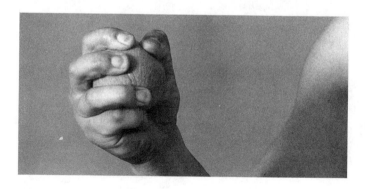

Squeeze a small object (2-3A)

2-4 Stick twist   i e

Correct execution: 1. Grasp a staff or stick in the middle with one hand. 2. Rotate your hand and forearm to the right and left while keeping your upper arm stationary.

Main benefit: Strengthens the hand, wrist and forearm

Martial arts applications: A strong forearm, wrist and grip are important in weapons practice as well as in throwing and striking techniques.

1. Grasp a stick   2. Rotate to the right

2-5 Hand stand push-ups   i p g

Correct execution: 1. Assume a hand stand position and have a partner hold your legs in the air. 2. Slowly lower yourself by flexing your elbows then push your body back up to the hand stand by straightening your arms.

Variation: **2-5A** If you do not have a partner, lean your feet against a wall for balance.

Main benefit: Strengthens arms, shoulders and chest

Also improves: balance, agility

Martial arts applications: Strengthens upper body muscles for striking, throwing and falling

Cautions: Always use a strong support so you don't lose your balance and drop your full body weight on your head and neck.

1. Start Position   2. Flex position

2-6 Chin-ups   i   e

Correct execution: 1. Grasp the chinning bar with your palms facing out. 2. Hang with your knees bent and your arms extended. 3. Pull yourself up with your arms until your chin is above the bar then return to the starting position.

Variations: **2-6A** Grasp the bar with your palms facing you
                    2-6B Hanging on the bar, pull your knees up to your chest

Main benefit: Strengthens arms and shoulders

Martial arts applications: Strengthens upper body muscles for striking, throwing and falling.

1. Grasp the bar, palms facing out and pull your body up (2-6)

Knee raise (2-6B)

2-7 Curl-ups   i g

Correct execution: 1. Lie on your back with your knees bent and your feet flat on the floor. 2. Place your hands on your chest and raise your chest slowly until your shoulder blades are off the floor. 3. Hold for five seconds then return to the starting position.

Variations: **2-7A** Curl-up and twist to the right and left alternately
                    2-7B Lift your feet off the floor, draw knees to your chest

Main benefit: Strengthens stomach muscles

Martial arts applications: Strong stomach muscles are essential for coordinating upper and lower body power and for mobilizing the leg for high kicks.

1. START: Lie back with knees bent

2. Lift your chest off the floor

Curl-up to the side (2-7A)

Lift your knees to your chest (2-7B)

2-8 V-ups   i g

Correct execution: 1. Lie on your back with your legs straight and your arms stretched over your head. 2. Raise your legs and arms simultaneously to a V position (touch your hands to your feet) then return to the starting position.

Main benefit: Strengthens back and stomach muscles

Also improves: agility, balance

Martial arts applications: Strong stomach and back muscles aid in total body movement and withstanding body blows.

Cautions: Stop if you experience back pain.

1. START: Lie back, hands above your head

2. Raise your arms and legs
simultaneously to a "V" position

2-9 Side sit-ups

Correct execution: 1. Lie on your side and have your partner hold your ankles on the floor. 2. Raise your upper body toward your feet then return to the starting position.

Main benefit: Strengthens oblique (side) muscles

Also improves: agility

Martial arts applications: Strong trunk muscles aid in upper and lower body coordination, jumping and spinning.

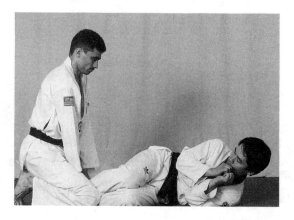

1. START: Lie on your side with your partner holding your ankles

2. Raise your upper body off the floor toward your partner

2-10 Back extensions   i p g

Correct execution: 1. Lie on your stomach with your hands clasped behind your head. 2. Raise your upper body off the floor, then lower it.

Variations: **2-10A** Stretch your arms out to the side
                    2-10B Stretch your arms over your head
                    2-10C Put your hands on your lower back
                    2-10D Raise your feet and arms at the same time

Main benefit: Strengthens back muscles

Martial arts applications: Strong stomach and back muscles aid in total body movement.

Back extension with feet raised (2-10D)

2-11 Trunk lifts   i g

Correct execution: 1. Kneel with your thighs perpendicular to the floor, your upper body leaning slightly forward and your hands behind your head. 2. Lean your upper body forward to six inches above the floor. 3. Return to the starting position.

Main benefit: Strengthens back

Martial arts applications: Strong back muscles improve throwing and takedowns

1. START: Kneel with thighs perpendicular to the floor and body slightly forward

2. Lean your upper body forward to within 6 inches of the floor.

2-12 Side leg raises   i g

Correct execution: 1. Lie on your side with your legs extended. 2. Lift your top leg up toward the ceiling then lower it.

Variations: **2-13A** Lift both legs simultaneously.
                    2-13B Lift one knee
                    2-13C Lift both knees

Main benefit: Strengthens trunk and leg muscles

Martial arts applications: Strong trunk and leg muscles aid in kicking skills

Lift one leg (2-12)

Lift both legs (2-12A)

Lift one knee (2-12B)

Lift both knees (2-12C)

2-13 Leg raises   i p g e

Correct execution: 1. Lie on your back with your legs straight. 2. Raise both legs until they point at the ceiling. 3. Then lower both legs to the floor.

Main benefit: Strengthens trunk and leg muscles

Also improves: coordination, flexibility

Martial arts applications: Strong trunk and leg muscles improve kicking

Variations: **2-12A** Alternate leg raises - Raise one leg at a time
2-12B Knee raises - Raise your knees simultaneously
2-12C Alternate knee raises - Raise one knee at a time

Raise both legs (2-13)

Raise one leg (2-13A)

Raise both knees (2-13B)

Raise one knee (2-13C)

2-12D Scissors - Lift both legs off the floor and cross and uncross them horizontally in a scissor motion.

2-12E Flutter kicks - Raise both legs 6 inches off the ground and alternately raise each leg to about 18 inches

2-12F Trunk twist - Raise both legs and then touch them to the floor on the side of your body.

2-12G With partner - Your partner stands near your head. When you raise your legs, he lightly pushes them back to the floor. Try to rebound as quickly as possible. He can also push them at a forty-five degree angle to the side.

2-12H Lie on a bench and lower your feet below the level of your hips then raise them.

Scissors (2-13D)

Flutter kicks (2-13E)

Trunk Twist (2-13F)

2-14 Knee-ups   i g

Correct execution: Standing, raise one knee to your chest then return to a standing position.

Main benefit: Strengthens leg and trunk muscles

Also improves: speed, coordination

Martial arts applications: Strengthens kicking initiation movements

1. START: Stand in a relaxed position.   2. Raise one knee to your chest.

2-15 Standing jump   i g

Correct execution: Standing next to a wall, jump straight up and touch the wall.

Variations: **2-15A** Draw a measuring stick on the wall to check jumping heights
2-15B Mark the wall with chalk on each jump

Main benefit: Strengthens legs

Also improves: speed, coordination, balance

Martial arts applications: Improves jumping kicks

1. START: Stand next to the wall   2. Jump and touch the wall

2-16 Lunges   i g e

Correct execution: 1. Stand with the feet slightly spread apart. 2. Step forward with one foot into a deep stance then return to the starting position.

Variation: **2-16A** Hold a barbell over your shoulders for increased weight.

Main benefit: Strengthens leg muscles

Also improves: flexibility

Martial arts applications: Strengthens the large muscle groups of the legs that are used in creating strong, deep stances and dynamic footwork.

Cautions: If you have pain in your knee during this exercise, bend less deeply and reduce the load. If the pain continues, stop this exercise.

Step forward with one foot (2-16)   Holding a barbell (2-16A)

2-17 Squats   i g e

Correct execution: From a standing position, slowly lower your body and flex your knees and then stand upright again.

Variation: **2-17A** Hold a barbell over your shoulders for added weight.

Main benefit: Strengthens legs

Martial arts applications: Improves kicking strength and stance stability.

Cautions: If you have knee pain, do not bend beyond ninety degrees.

Slowly flex your knees (2-17)

With Barbell (2-17A)

2-18 Calf raises   i g

Correct execution: 1. Stand flat on your feet and raise your body up onto your toes. 2. Hold for a few seconds and return to a standing position.

Variation: **2-18A** Hold a barbell over your shoulders for added weight.

Main benefit: Strengthens feet and ankles

Also improves: Balance, flexibility

Martial arts applications: Strong feet and ankles make strong stances and quick, sure footwork

Stand up on your toes and hold

With barbell (2-18A)

TRACKING YOUR PROGRESS

Select one exercise from each of the above groups and track your progress with each workout. You may make copies of this page for future use.

1. Neck, arms, shoulders group: #2-1 through #2-6
   Exercise _____

DATE	REPS	SETS	WEIGHT

TRACKING YOUR PROGRESS

2. Chest, back, abdomen group: #2-7 through #2-11
     Exercise _____

DATE	REPS	SETS	WEIGHT

TRACKING YOUR PROGRESS

3. Buttocks, legs group: # 2-12 through # 2-18
     Exercise _____

DATE	REPS	SETS	WEIGHT

INSTRUCTOR'S NOTES

① Structure group strength training according to class or belt level. For beginners, start with a minimum number of repetitions. As students progress in belt level, increase the number of repetitions and eventually the number of sets of each exercise. It is not necessary to tell students the number of exercises at each level. Just lead the class and encourage students to complete each set.

② If you have a class that has a wide range of levels, work to the upper-middle range of the class. Encourage lower level students to follow, but do not require them to complete every set perfectly. Another strategy is to set a time limit, like one minute, and let everyone complete as many of the exercise as they can in that period. Advanced students complete each exercise more quickly than beginners, finishing more repetitions in the same amount of time.

③ Carefully observe the cautions related to each exercise and clearly communicate them when you introduce an exercise that is new to students. Many people are not in good shape when they begin training and are susceptible to injuries due to improper technique or weight load.

3

SPEED

WHAT IS IT?

In strict mechanical terms, speed is defined as the distance covered divided by the time taken, as in fifty miles per hour or 100 feet per second. For our purposes however, these types of measures are almost meaningless. In martial arts, distance and time are not as important as being able to move faster than the opponent.

In a practical sense, speed is the ability to move the whole or any part of the body from one place to another in the shortest possible time. It is primarily an innate characteristic but it can be improved through training. Training for speed focuses on skill in technique and efficiency in movement. Speed at its most developed level is characterized by a high level of skill refinement in every action.

Overall movement or body speed is affected by several physiological factors:

Perception speed - Perception speed is the quickness with which you recognize that a response is demanded.

Example: Your opponent punches you and you respond by blocking. Before you can block his punch, your brain must first discern that a threat is impending and a response is immediately necessary.

Reaction speed - Reaction speed is the quickness with which you formulate and initiate a response.

Example: Once your brain determines that a response to your opponent's punch is necessary, it decides what response is most appropriate and sends the necessary signals to the appropriate body parts to initiate a response.

Execution speed - Execution speed is the quickness with which your body performs the actual response once it has been initiated.

Example: Your brain determines that a high section block is necessary and signals your arm and upper body to move in the pattern of a high section block. The speed with which your arm and body are able to respond to this demand is the execution speed.

Recovery speed - Recovery speed is the quickness of your return to a state of readiness.

Example: When you complete the high section block, you have to return your arm to a guard position and ready your body for the next required action.

Perception, reaction, execution and recovery speed can all be improved through practice. You begin to notice changes in speed in a few weeks, but the real gains take about one year as your body and brain become acclimated to a new standard of movement. Consistent, intensive training is the fastest route to speed development. Remember, speed is different from being in a hurry. Speed requires trained and precise movement.

WHERE DOES IT COME FROM?

Speed is primarily derived from the adeptness of the nervous system and quickness of muscular contraction. Perception and reaction speed rely on the quick response of the visual and nervous systems. First, your eyes or in some cases your ears perceive the need for a response. Next, they rapidly and accurately transmit the nature of the event requiring the response to the brain. The brain compares this event with similar, previously experienced circumstances and searches for an appropriate response.

Once a response is selected, the brain sends out signals to the body via the nervous system. The body responds to these intricate commands. During the execution period, the brain and body communicate to make minute adjustments in every phase of the movement. When the body finishes its designated course of action, it relaxes and returns to its pre-activity state. This entire process can take place hundreds of times a minute as your body reads and adapts to its changing environment.

HOW DOES IT APPLY TO MARTIAL ARTS?

Speed can save you from being hit and allow you to out-hit your opponent. It is the key to winning when you and your opponent are equal in technical ability. Speed is essential if you are small and want to defeat a larger opponent. Speed is the way to maximize the power of a technique, especially when you peak in your strength training. Remember, speed is the second component of power.

HOW TO IMPROVE

To develop overall speed, there are several sequential steps in training:

1. Basic conditioning
2. Explosive power development
3. Skill refinement
4. Skill loading
5. Full speed training

Basic condition, including flexibility, strength and agility training, is a prerequisite for speed training. The completion of basic conditioning is signaled by a level of fitness that allows the athlete to begin the more intensive exercises that develop explosive power. Exercises for developing explosive power are detailed in "Chapter 2: Power" and the execution speed section of this chapter. Once the target muscles start to develop, begin working on skill refinement. Each skill should be examined to eliminate unnecessary movements and increase biomechanical efficiency.

With highly refined movements and strong muscles, you can begin adding speed to each movement. Start skill loading gradually and observe your body's reaction. If you can add speed and still maintain semi-refined movements, continue to increase your intensity. Eventually you will reach the final stage of speed training in which you can execute skillful movements at high speed.

Now let's examine the four types of speed individually.

Perception speed can be increased by repeatedly exposing yourself to situations that require instant analysis. Law enforcement officers do this by participating in mock confrontations that require them to quickly analyze who demands to be responded to and how. The best drill for developing perception speed in martial artists is sparring.

Sparring teaches you what an attack looks like before it happens. Sparring also teaches you to be alert at all times by placing you in imminent physical danger. Alertness is one of the keys to perception speed. You cannot analyze the situation if you do not realize it exists.

Reaction speed is improved by a two pronged approach. First, you have to be aware of what types of situations may arise in any given environment. In sparring, your opponent does one of several things which are predetermined by the rules of the sparring match. You know in advance what is allowed and what is not.

In a self-defense situation, you also have some idea what to expect. You can reasonably expect your assailant to try to harm you in some way. You do not expect him to start singing songs or reciting poetry. By estimating what to expect from the given environment, you narrow down your choice of possible responses.

Second, you have to have experienced an identical or similar situation before. If you have been attacked hundreds of times by a front kick in sparring, your reaction becomes almost reflexive. If you are sparring for the first time, your reaction time is longer because you must formulate a response without a basis for comparison. If you have practiced self-defense techniques in a realistic way hundreds of times, you are much more well prepared than if you spend all of your time beating up a stationary heavy bag.

Execution speed is the type of speed that most martial arts training focuses on. Executing techniques like kicks and punches with speed takes up a large part of the intermediate and advanced stages of training. Execution speed can best be improved through attention to detail. Shifting into a ready posture at the last minute wastes time. Begin each movement with a ready and relaxed posture.   If you are going to punch, have your hands up and ready. If you are going to kick, shift your weight to supporting leg and relax your kicking leg. Shifting your weight and positioning your hands can take more time than the actual striking or kicking. Anticipate what is necessary and be prepared.

When you learn a new skill, practice slowly at first to train your muscles in the correct execution of the movement. When you can execute with little thought about the segments of the movement, speed up gradually.   In speeding up the movement, take care not to loose the precision you learned in the beginner stage. Strong basics are essential for speed training.

Observing the laws of motion is also important to execution speed.   If you flail your arms and head wildly about when kicking, your kick will be slow. If you stabilize your posture, your kicking speed will increase. If you punch with your arm, your punching will be slow. If you punch from your hips, your punching speed and power will increase. If you spin with your upper body tilted to one side, you will lose your balance and fall. If you spin with your upper body fixed as the axis of your movement, you will spin smoothly and quickly.

Every technique has a correct application that takes into account the laws of motion and enables you to take the shortest possible route to your target. Every skill also has complementary and noncomplementary skills to combine with it. Combining a jumping side kick with an axe kick does nothing to improve the speed of either. Combining a roundhouse kick with a back kick, however, creates a continuous circle of whirling force, increasing the speed of the second kick.

Finally, relax to create speed. Tense muscles have more difficulty responding to your intense demands than relaxed muscles. Relax just prior to the movement and maintain a minimum amount of tension during the movement. Relaxation conserves energy and lessens the amount of force necessary to move your body quickly.

Recovery speed is the result of execution speed. The old adage "what goes up must come down" applies in other directions as well. If your fist shoots out in a punching motion, it must return along the same path to be efficient and effective. If you execute a side kick and drop your leg to the ground immediately following impact, you will be off balance and in danger. You must rechamber the leg and then return to a natural stance.

If you do not execute the recovery portion of the technique, the action becomes "dead." It does not have the dynamic quality associated with speedy movement. It also increases the risk of joint injury tremendously. A fast strike or kick that ends in a locked out position is a common case of knee and elbow injuries.

A complete technique has an initiation, execution, impact and recovery. Each phase must be executed correctly to create dynamic speed.

CAUTIONS

❖ Never use complex skills for speed training.

❖ Always master the basics before moving to speed training.

❖ Never tense your muscles before executing a speed skill.

❖ Muscles must be well trained before engaging in speed training. Weak muscles that cannot bear the intense requirements of speed training are be easily injured.

3-1 Initiation drill   i g

Correct execution: Select a simple movement that you want to execute faster. Isolate the initiation movement, that is the movement that takes place as you begin to execute the skill. (Example: To improve front kick, start with the knee cocking motion. To improve roundhouse kick, start with the hip insertion. To improve back kick start with the pivot.) Practice the initiation movement as quickly as possible. When you have a speedy initiation segment, let the rest of the skill flow from it.

Main benefit: Decreases reaction time

Also improves: timing, coordination

Martial arts applications: Increases the speed of individual skills

1. Begin in ready stance   2. Front kick initiation movement

3-2 Relax and Focus drill   i g

Correct execution: 1. Fully relax your arm. 2. From a state of total relaxation, explode with a jab.

Variation: **3-2A** Can be used for any skill by consciously relaxing the target muscles then creating an explosive initiation movement

Main benefit: Increases reaction speed

Also improves: timing, coordination, power

Martial arts applications: Increases the speed of initiation from a relaxed state

1. Assume a relaxed ready stance

2. Execute an explosive jab

3-3 Whistle drill   i g e

Correct execution: One person performs a simple footwork drill like sliding to the right. When his partner blows a whistle, he quickly switches to sliding to the left. Allow one to five steps between whistles.

Variations: **3-3A** In a group, one person blows the whistle while the others practice.
3-3B Also works with sliding forward/backward and stepping forward/backward

Main benefit: Increases reaction speed

Also improves: agility, coordination, balance

Martial arts applications: Increases footwork speed and decreases response time

Cautions: Quick changes in direction can cause ankle and knee injuries

Sliding side to side (3-3)

3-4 Bounding   i g

Correct execution: Leap forward with long, bounding strides.

Variation: **3-4A** Move side to side with bounding strides

Main benefit: Improves execution speed

Also improves: power, balance, agility

Martial arts applications: Improves speed in footwork

Cautions: Do not do this exercise if you have a knee or ankle injury

Lateral bounding (3-4A)

3-5 Sprinting

Correct execution: Mark off a distance from 10 to 50 yards. Run the distance as quickly as possible. Focus on increasing speed with every step.

Variations: **3-5A** Races - Race against a partner of similar skill level to push yourself harder.
3-5B Relay races - In a group of people, organize relay races with up to four people on each team. Each person sprints the marked distance, turns and sprints back to tag the next person in line. The first team to finish wins.
3-5C Timed sprints - Ask a partner to time your sprint. Try to improve your time on a weekly basis.

Main benefit: Improves leg speed

Also improves: strength, endurance

Martial arts applications: Strong, fast leg muscles improve kicking, jumping, stances and footwork. Improved anaerobic energy production enhances short, intense activities such as those required in sparring and ground combat. The mental intensity of sprinting is similar to that of combat.

3-6 Uphill running

Correct execution: Sprint 30 to 100 yards uphill. To increase your speed, look at the top of the incline and lean your body slightly backwards. Jog or walk down the hill.

Variations: **3-6A** Run up stairs
                      3-6B If you do not have an incline, run in sand.

Main benefit: Improves explosive leg speed

Also improves: endurance, power

Martial arts applications: Explosive leg speed increases the initiation and execution speed for kicking, footwork and throwing

Cautions: Running downhill places extraordinary stress on the leg muscles and joints. Use the downhill jog or walk as a recovery period.

3-7 Speed drill with target   p g e

Correct execution: Select a simple skill like punching or front kick. Using a target or heavy bag, execute the technique as many times as you can in thirty or sixty seconds.

Variations: **3-7A** Add footwork to the movement
              3-7B Count only those strikes that hit the target correctly

Main benefit: Increases execution speed

Also improves: endurance, timing, coordination, agility, accuracy

Martial arts applications: Increases the speed of each skill as well as the transition speed between skills. Excellent drill for sparring.

Cautions: Avoid using complex skills like jumping or spinning kicks.

Kick and strike the target while your partner varies the height

3-8 Obstacle jump   i g e

Correct execution: 1. Place a heavy bag lying down on the floor and stand next to it. 2. Jump over it, side to side, with both feet together.

Variations: **3-8A** Use a higher and\or wider object as you progress
3-8B Instead of jumping over the object, jump onto and off of it

Main benefit: Improves execution speed in leg skills

Also improves: power, agility, coordination

Martial arts applications: Improves leg speed and explosive jumping kicks

Caution: If you have a knee or ankle injury, do not use this exercise.

Jump over and obstacle (3-8)

3-9 Water training   i e

Correct execution: In a pool or body of water where you can stand firmly on the bottom, practice executing skills you want to improve. The water provides consistent resistance throughout the natural range of motion. This strengthens the recovery response which is often ignored in other training exercises. Water training is an excellent rehabilitation exercise for joint injuries.

Main benefit: improves recovery speed

Also improves: endurance, power

Martial arts applications: Practicing a movement with resistance through the full range of motion increases the speed of the movement in both the execution and recovery period.

Cautions: Always practice water training with adequate supervision.

3-10 Bicycle Tube drill   i g e

Correct execution: Cut a bicycle tube so it forms a single length. Fix one end so it is stationary. Hold the other end in your hand and practice hand striking techniques. Resist the pull of the tube during the recovery phase of the movement.

Variation: **3-10A** Tie the tube to your ankle and practice kicking.

Main benefit: strengthens the flexor muscles

Also improves: power

Martial arts applications: Increases the resistance during the recovery phase to develop a more powerful recovery movement.

Cautions: Fast or jerky movements may result in joint injuries.

Punching with bicycle tube (3-10)   Kicking with bicycle tube (3-10A)

TRACKING YOUR PROGRESS

The following exercises are suggested for tracking your progress with each workout. Under time, record only the best time you score during your workout on that day. You may make copies of this page for future use.

Sprinting (3-5)

DATE	DISTANCE	BEST TIME

TRACKING YOUR PROGRESS

Uphill run (#3-6)

DATE	DISTANCE	BEST TIME

TRACKING YOUR PROGRESS

Speed drill with target (#3-7)

DATE	SKILL	REPS	BEST TIME

INSTRUCTOR'S NOTES

① Speed training is recommended for intermediate and advanced level students. If you emphasize speed training before the students' fundamental skills are solid, they will become easily frustrated and their technique will be sloppy.

② Speed training should be accompanied by a strength training program for the corresponding muscles.

4

PERCEPTION

WHAT IS IT?

Perception is the ongoing cerebral process of organizing and giving meaning to sensory input.   Our perception of events and situations determines the responses that we make to the world around us. Effective and efficient responses in both learning and performance are highly dependent on perception.

Perception is often lessened or blocked by fatigue, emotion, lack of mental conditioning, lack of training, inattention to detail, and preoccupation with extraneous stimuli.

No two people perceive an object or event the same way. Some people perceive whole ideas and scenes at one time while others prefer to break things into segments. Some people prefer visual perception while others prefer tactile perception. Many people combine or switch between the two. To improve your perception skills, identify what style works best for you and capitalize on it.

WHERE DOES IT COME FROM?

Perception is the first step in the action chain. Before you can respond to an event, you must perceive that a response is necessary. There are four classes of perception:

Detection - Detection is the realization of a stimulus.
Discrimination - Discrimination is the ability to differentiate between types of stimuli.
Recognition - Recognition is an awareness of the familiarity of an object.
Identification - Identification is the ability to select an appropriate response to a stimulus.

Example: During a sparring match, your opponent throws a punch at your stomach. First, you must realize that he is taking an action that requires you to respond (detection). Next, you have to choose between the action that requires your attention and other extraneous actions he is using to distract you (discrimination). Then you have to recognize what that key action is by comparing it with similar movements you have seen or experienced before (recognition). Finally, you have to select the best response to his action (identification).

HOW DOES IT APPLY TO MARTIAL ARTS?

Perception is a basic requirement for the acquisition of physical skills. When you learn a new skill, your brain categorizes it based on what you have previously learned. Assume you know how to punch. When you learn to punch while moving forward, your brain relates the two skills as similar. Your ability to recognize the similarities between known and new skills significantly speeds the learning process. By accurately organizing and defining incoming information, you can translate new concepts into physical action.

Perception is significant in skills that require a variable response such as sparring and self-defense, and less important in individual skills like kicking and striking practice. When you interact with another person, your brain organizes and responds to hundreds of minute details. With a low level of perception, you observe and respond to only the most obvious sensory cues.

With a high level of perception, you can focus on every aspect of your partner or opponent's action, giving you an advantage in responding quickly and accurately. Practice cuing in on habits and subtle changes in your opponent's demeanor. Remember to notice auditory as well as visual cues. Your response to auditory cues, such as your opponent's shouts or threats, may be quicker than a visually based response.

HOW TO IMPROVE

Since perception is largely a process of recognition and response, the best way to improve it is to experience situations that model your target activity. By simulating the target activity, you learn to recognize common movements or movement patterns more quickly. You can understand the meanings of the movements and formulate responses with less thought than if you had not previously experienced them. Your reactions are quicker when they do not require making complex choices.

A second way of improving is to develop a high level of fundamental skill. Select a limited number of simple skills and practice them to perfection. If you do not have to devote your thought process to remembering how to punch, you can respond with a counter punch much quicker than an inexperienced fighter.

Example: If you know that a common counterattack to a right leg roundhouse kick is a right leg roundhouse kick and you practice this response, it becomes automatic. When you see a right leg roundhouse kick, you respond instinctively. If you do not know and practice this specific formula, you may respond with a right roundhouse kick one time, a block and punch another time and a front kick yet another time. Each successive response takes time to formulate and further complicates the next response.

Practice and knowledge are the keys to heightening your perception.

4-1 Jumping spin   i g

Correct execution: Standing, raise your right arm and spin 360 degrees to your right. Then raise your left arm and spin 360 degrees to your left. Try to land in the same spot where you began.

Variation: **4-1A** If you can spin 360 degrees easily try one and a half or two full spins.

Main benefit: Improves spatial perception

Also improves: balance

Martial arts applications: Teaches you to understand your body's relationship to your environment while in motion. Mobile space perception is important in forms performance and in perceiving your surroundings in sparring and close combat.

1. Raise your right arm   2. Jump and spin

4-2 Standing spin   i g

Correct execution: Spin ten to fifteen times in a circle then immediately try to walk on a straight line.

Main benefit: Improves spatial perception

Also improves: coordination, balance

Martial arts applications: Lessens dizziness during spinning skills and helps in recovery after spinning techniques.

Cautions: Practice in an open area free of obstacles and sharp objects.

4-3 Dodge ball   g e

Correct execution: Make a big circle with one person standing at the center. The people in the circle throw a soft ball at the center person, trying to hit him below the shoulders. Whoever succeeds in hitting him takes his place.

Variations: **4-3A** Use more than one person in the center and/or more than one ball
4-3B Stand in opposing lines instead of a circle

Main benefit: Improves spatial perception

Also improves: agility, speed

Martial arts benefit: Improves evasion and footwork skills

Cautions: To minimize the risk of injury, limit targets to below the knees for children

4-4 Sweep jumps p g e

Correct execution: 1. Partner A holds a belt and Partner B stands about three feet from him. 2. Partner A spins in a circle dragging the belt just above the floor. 3. As the belt approaches, partner B jumps over it.

Variations: **4-4A** Vary the speed of spinning
4-4B Use two belts, one in each hand
4-4C Wiggle the belt unpredictably
4-4D Vary the height of the belt
4-4E Swing the belt at head height and duck under it

Main benefit: Improves spatial perception

Also improves: agility, coordination, timing

Martial arts applications: Improves reaction time and reaction selection

Cautions: When swinging the belt at head height, wear eye and ear protection.

4-5 Form practice with eyes closed   i g

Correct execution: Close your eyes and practice a form with emphasis on moving in the correct direction. In the beginning, you can open you eyes periodically to check that you are moving in the correct direction and make any necessary adjustments.

Variation: 4-5A With your eyes closed, try to execute a combination of skills while moving on a straight line

Main benefit: Improves spatial perception

Also improves: coordination, balance

Martial arts applications: Improves your ability to move in relationship to your environment without relying on visual perception.   Improving your nonvisual perception increases your awareness of your surroundings.

Cautions: Always practice with a partner and only in an area free of obstacles and sharp objects.

4-6 Retrieval   i g e

Correct execution: Throw a small object like a shoe, close your eyes and retrieve it.

Main benefit: Distance perception by memory

Martial arts applications: Teaches you to judge distance by memory only.

Cautions: Always practice with a partner and only in an area free of obstacles and sharp objects.

4-7 Blind retrieval   i g e

Correct execution: Close your eyes and throw a small object. Without looking, retrieve it.

Main benefit: Improves distance perception through sound

Martial arts applications: Teaches you to judge distance by sound only, a skill necessary for fighting in dark or poorly lit areas.

Cautions: Always practice with a partner and only in an area free of obstacles and sharp objects.

4-8 Counter Attack Response Drill   p g

Correct execution: Stand facing a partner at about arm's length. One partner attacks with a variety of hand strikes and the other blocks accordingly. Begin with a limited number of techniques and gradually work up to a free exchange.

Variations: **4-8A** Can also be applied to kicking, locking and throwing attacks depending on the art you practice.
4-8B Can be done in a group by having one person stand in the center of the circle and others randomly take turns attacking him.

Main benefit: Improves differentiation and identification skills

Also improves: coordination, accuracy, timing

Martial arts applications: Improves your ability to recognize and respond appropriately to a wide variety of attacks.

Cautions: Use light contact and adequate protection gear.

4-9 Target response   p g e

Correct execution: One partner holds a hand target and randomly presents it for the other partner to strike with a predesignated strike or kick.

Variations: **4-9A** Target holder varies the timing of the presentation
4-9B Target holder withdraws the target after 2 to 5 seconds depending on the skill level of the attacker
4-9C Target holder presents different target positions to indicate different strikes or kicks (i.e. straight for front kick, to the side for side kick and head high for punching)
4-9D Can be done in a group by having one person stand in the center of a circle of people and randomly present the target around the circle.

Main benefit: Improves detection and identification

Also improves: timing, accuracy, speed

Martial arts applications: By varying the timing and type of target opportunities presented, you improve your ability to recognize and respond quickly to simulated openings.

1. The holder presents the target   2. The attacker quickly strikes it

4-10 Night Tag   p g

Correct execution: Partners stand facing each other at arm's length. Partner A closes his eyes and Partner B tags him somewhere on his body. Partner B then tries to evade while Partner A tries to tag him back. Partner B continues tagging and evading at random intervals. Partner A must stay in one spot and move only his upper body, but Partner B may move anywhere.

Main benefit: Improves tactile perception

Also improves: speed, timing

Martial arts applications: Learning to respond quickly based on touch is a key skill in contact sparring and grappling contests.

Cautions: Use light contact and wear protection gear where necessary.

4-11 Chalk sparring

Correct execution: Partners face each other in fighting stance. Each holds a piece of colored chalk in his right hand and tries to mark the other's uniform with his piece of chalk. The one with the lesser number of marks on his uniform at the end of the round is the winner.

Variation: 4-11A The first person to score a mark is the winner.

Main benefit: Improves perceptual speed

Also improves: speed, agility, coordination

Martial arts applications: Teaches quick responses to hand attacks in sparring.

Cautions: Use in a class situation on a voluntary basis. Some people won't approve of getting their uniform dirty.

TRACKING YOUR PROGRESS

1. Spatial Awareness   (Exercises #4-1 through 4-4)

Sweep jumps (#4-4)

Have your partner spin twenty rotations varying the speed and height of the belt. Count the number of times you successfully evade the belt. Increase the number of rotations as you improve.

DATE	NUMBER	DATE	NUMBER

TRACKING YOUR PROGRESS

2. Nonvisual perception (Exercises # 4-5 through 4-7)

Retrieval (#4-6)

With the retrieval or blind retrieval drill, use a stopwatch to time how long it takes for you to successfully retrieve the object.

DATE	TIME	DATE	TIME

TRACKING YOUR PROGRESS

3. Perceptual speed (Exercises #4-8 through 4-11)

Target response (#4-9)

Have your partner present you with twenty consecutive, random targets. Count the number of times you respond correctly and accurately. Divide the number of hits by the number of attempts to find your success percentage. (e.g. 10 hits out of 20 attempts = 10 divided by 20 = .50 or 50%) As you improve increase the number of attempts per set to thirty, forty or even fifty.

DATE	ATTEMPTS	HITS	%

INSTRUCTOR'S NOTES

① Many of the above perception drills require students to close their eyes or in some way be deprived of their usual avenues of perception. Supervise theses activities carefully and pair students with partners who can guide them if necessary.

② Allow plenty of space between students and groups of students for perception drills.

③ Perception drills are unique and add a fun element to class while providing valuable lessons, especially for children's classes. After drill practice, illustrate how the drill applies to sparring or self-defense techniques.

5

COORDINATION

WHAT IS IT?

Coordination is the ability to integrate physical and psychological processes into an efficient pattern of movement. It is vital to success in most physical activities especially those that require eye-hand, eye-foot and rhythmic movements. Coordination plays a major role in agility development.

WHERE DOES IT COME FROM?

Coordination comes from the integration of physical skills like balance, speed and timing, with the sensory input of the visual, tactile and auditory systems. Integration requires developing from thinking about each attribute separately to functioning as a unified body.

Once a skill is learned, as through practice, the brain relies less on sensory input and more on the programmed execution of skills. Imagine learning to drive a car with a manual shift. You have to concentrate on letting out the clutch while depressing the gas pedal at just the right time to begin moving forward. At first, the coordination of the clutch, brake and gas pedal can be mind boggling.

With practice, you learn the timing of the clutch-gas interplay and your brain forms a set program to execute every time a shift is required. Soon, shifting is almost an unconscious act.

Through repetition, almost any movement can undergo this transformation. By repeating a skill, you signal the brain to create a programmed response to the demand for that skill. This is known as learning.

HOW DOES IT APPLY TO MARTIAL ARTS?

Martial arts movements place heavy emphasis on total body movement. To create total body movement, your individual body parts must be able to synchronize with each other and as a whole. There are also many martial arts movements that strike a target. Kicking a target requires eye-foot coordination and striking a target requires eye-hand coordination.

Combination movements, like punch-kick combinations require coordination between the limbs and the trunk. Throwing applications require coordination of the upper and lower body. There are many other types of coordination found in martial arts movements: right-left, left-right, up-down, down-up, front-back, back-front, angular right-angular left, angular left-angular-right, circular, spinning, etc. Pinpoint the types of coordination required in the style you practice and focus on the exercises best suited for the enhancement you need.

HOW TO IMPROVE

Coordination, like agility, is something you can improve only through experience. By practicing movements and exercises that require coordination, you develop an awareness of what coordination feels like.

If the coordination exercises are too difficult, work on basic skills like middle punch and front kick. By practicing a limited spectrum of skills repeatedly, your minimum level of aptitude increases. Once you can execute simple skills, add one element, like a step forward. When you can step forward and punch well, add another movement, like left step forward, right punch and right front kick. When you can handle a simple combination, add speed and power.

Work at your own pace, no matter how slow. Concentrate on developing a few skills well, especially the fundamental techniques of the style you practice. Once you get the feel of doing something well, you have a basis for learning more complex skills.

Before you begin a new skill, especially a complicated one, visualize it. See yourself performing as well as your instructor or someone else who has excellent coordination. Imagine how your body will move when you are perfectly coordinated.

After you visualize yourself, try to imitate what you imagined, with more emphasis on the feeling you felt during the visualization than on perfecting the mechanics of the movement. Coordination starts with your brain and flows through your body. Develop a feeling for coordinated movements that you can transfer from one new skill to the next.

5-1 Jumping Jacks   i g

Correct execution: 1. Stand with your feet together and your hands at your sides. 2. Jump and land with your feet shoulder distance apart and your palms touching above your head. 3. Jump and return to the starting position.

Variations: **5-1A** Cross your feet instead of putting them together.
5-1B Move your feet alternately forward and backward instead of to the side

Main benefit: Total body coordination

Also improves: endurance

Martial arts applications: Develops the upper and lower body coordination necessary for almost every martial arts movement.

5-2 Jumping Rope   i e

Correct execution: Jump with both feet together each time the rope makes one rotation.

Variations: **5-2A** Alternate feet
5-2B Hop on one foot
5-2C Cross your hands in front of you on every other rotation
5-2D Spin two rotations per jump
5-2E Spin the rope backwards so it approaches your feet from behind and use any of the above types of jumping

Main benefit: Hand-eye and hand-foot coordination

Also improves: timing, endurance

Martial arts applications: Improves sparring rhythm and combination skills

5-3 Knee touch

Correct execution: Lift your right knee up to your chest and simultaneously hop forward on your left leg, using the force of your right knee to carry your body forward. Alternate legs while moving forward across the floor.

Main benefit: Improves coordination

Also improves: balance, agility

Martial arts applications: Improves your ability to move your entire body together while balancing on one leg and maintaining your center of gravity. Good for sliding and skipping attacks.

Lift your knee and slide forward

5-4 Side scoop   i g

Correct execution: Jog forward and reach down with your right hand to scoop the ground on your right side. Then use your left hand on your left side.

Main benefit: Improves high-low coordination

Also improves: agility, balance

Martial arts applications: Improves your ability to change heights in grappling and throwing.

Scoop the ground with your hand

5-5 Between belt jumps

Correct execution: 1. Two people hold one belt at their knee level and one at their shoulder level. 2. Other participants try to jump between the belts without touching them. 3. Move the belts closer together with each successive try.

Main benefit: Upper and lower body coordination

Also improves: agility

Martial arts applications: Improves the ability to avoid obstacles with the upper and lower body simultaneously. Good practice for self-defense.

5-6 Star jumps   i g

Correct execution: 1. Squat and then jump up, extending your arms and legs into a star shape. 2. Land and return to a squatting position.

Main benefit: Total body coordination

Also improves: speed, strength, agility, balance

Martial arts applications: Improves coordination during sudden, speedy movements.

1. Squat

2. Jump and extend your arms and legs

5-7 Forward Roll   i g

Correct execution: Place your hands on the ground, tuck your chin to your chest and roll in a tuck position.

Variation: **5-7A** After you roll, immediately jump up with your arms extended over your head.

Main benefit: Total body coordination

Martial arts applications: Improves falling and recovery skills

Cautions: Use caution and work on an impact absorbing surface to prevent head, neck and spine injuries.

1. START: Squat in a tuck position.

2. Roll forward

5-8 Backward Roll   i g

Correct execution: 1. Squat and place your hands next to your head with palms facing up. 2. Drop your hips to the floor and roll over backwards, using your hands to help you roll.

Main benefit: Total body coordination

Martial arts applications: Good for falling and recovery skills

Cautions: Use caution and work on an impact absorbing surface to prevent head, neck, spine and finger injuries. Always tuck your chin to your chest during back falls to prevent hitting your head on the floor.

1. START: Squat in a tuck position.

2. Roll backward.

5-9 Partner back rolls   p g

Correct execution: 1. Partners squat facing each other with their palms touching. 2. On cue, each pushes off and rolls backwards and then quickly returns to the starting position.

Main benefit: Total body coordination

Also improves: balance, agility, flexibility

Martial arts applications: Improves falling and height changes in ground fighting applications.

Cautions: Always tuck your chin to your chest during a back fall to avoid hitting your head on the floor. Partners should apply only minimal pressure when pushing off.

1. START: Partners squat facing each other.

2. Both roll backward at the same time and return to the starting position.

5-10 Ball pass   p g e

Correct execution: 1. Both partners assume a shoulder standing position with their heads near each other and their feet pointing toward the ceiling. 2. Partner A balances a ball on his feet and passes it to Partner B. 3. Partner B flexes and straightens his knees with the ball and then passes it back to Partner A.

Main benefit: Lower body coordination

Also improves: balance, strength

Martial arts applications: Lower body sensitivity is essential for complex kicking and footwork.

5-11 Bicycling   i g

Correct execution: 1. Lie on your back and raise your hips. 2. Move your legs as if you were riding a bicycle.

Variations: **5-11A** Draw your knees in toward your chest and place your hands behind your head, elevating your shoulders off the floor.
5-11B Alternately pump your legs in and out while alternately twisting your elbows toward your knees.

Main benefit: Upper and lower body coordination

Also improves: strength, agility

Martial arts applications: Upper and lower body coordination aids in total body movements like footwork/striking combinations and throwing.

Bicycling (5-11)

Bicycling with shoulders raised (5-11A)

TRACKING YOUR PROGRESS

The following are some sample exercises through which you can track your progress. You may copy these pages for future use:

1. **Jumping Rope (#5-2)**

Count only consecutive error-free jumps. When you stop or make a mistake, start counting from number one again. Record your best number from each workout.

DATE	TYPE OF JUMP	# OF JUMPS

TRACKING YOUR PROGRESS

2. Ball Pass (#5-10)

Count the number of consecutive successful passes. Record the best number form each workout.

DATE	# OF PASSES	DATE	# OF PASSES

INSTRUCTOR'S NOTES

① Lack of coordination is often related to a lack of confidence in physical abilities. For uncoordinated students, divide combination movements into simple steps and stick to basic skills. By building up their body confidence, you make these students feel coordinated. Once they feel what it is like to be coordinated, they can transfer this feeling to more complex movements.

② One of the major hurdles for uncoordinated people is free sparring. No matter how hard they try, they end up tied in a knot and unable to respond quickly enough to their opponent. For these people, spend more time in arranged sparring drills. Make them feel comfortable with one or two techniques they can use to respond to a variety of attacks. When they can rely on a few familiar skills, they will relax in free sparring and thus be able to respond faster to their opponents.

③ Teenagers, especially boys, go through a period of awkwardness as they experience their growth spurt. When you see signs of confusion in a previously athletic boy or girl, reassure them that this is normal and that they must work through it. Give them some extra instruction on how to take advantage of their expanding size and how to mange their feelings of clumsiness.

6

BALANCE

WHAT IS IT?

Balance is the ability to maintain your body position and equilibrium both in movement and at rest.   There are two types of balance: static and dynamic. Static balance denotes a stationary object at equilibrium such as when you stand upright. Dynamic balance describes a body moving at constant linear and angular velocities. Because of the effects of gravity, dynamic balance is rarely found in our everyday life. A practical adaptation of dynamic balance could be called balance in motion, such as running and jumping.

WHERE DOES IT COME FROM?

The source of balance is found in two different realms of science: human physiology and biomechanics.

Physiological sources

Balance comes from good posture. By aligning your feet, hips, spine and head, you maintain a stable upright posture. To aid in balance, your body is equipped with special sensors to help you determine whether or not you are upright and aligned.

The most important sensors are the presence or lack of visual cues. Vision provides your body with a ready means of finding your position relative to the ground. To test the importance of vision, try closing your eyes and standing on one foot. You will feel your body sway and your arms reach out to the side instinctively.

Tactile cues are also used to maintain balance. In the pads of your feet are detailed networks of sensors. By sensing the pressure of the ground beneath them, they relay important information to the brain, allowing it to shift your balance as necessary. To test these, try standing on one foot on a soft surface like a mattress or thick mat. As the surface shifts beneath your weight, your body moves in response to the sensations transmitted from your foot pads.

Finally, there is the vestibular apparatus, found in the inner ear. It is made up of two kinds of receptors: semicircular canals that respond to angular movement and otolith organs that respond to linear movement. The vestibular apparatus is sensitive to the position of the head in space (upright or upside down) and to sudden changes in direction. Its primary function is to maintain equilibrium.

Through a highly sensitive sensory capacity, the vestibular apparatus allows the central nervous system to make balance adjustments, sometimes even before imbalance is felt. The vestibular apparatus also controls the "righting reflex," which takes precedence over other sensory and motor systems during disorientation.

The righting reflex controls upright posture. Based on input from the visual, tactile and vestibular senses, your body is constantly striving to maintain a specific orientation to gravity. When you lose your balance or become spatially disoriented, your righting reflex takes over to restore an upright posture by first positioning your head, followed by your neck and upper body and finally your lower body.

Biomechanical sources

The human body is equipped with a detailed physiological warning system in the event of imbalance. It makes every effort to maintain a continuous state of equilibrium. Physical forces like gravity, however, are in constant opposition. This is where an understanding of the biomechanical basis for equilibrium comes into play.

Every martial artist eventually hears the term "center of gravity" in relation to some movement. "Lower your center of gravity" is a common correction in the development of stances and footwork. But how many people know just where their center of gravity is and how to lower it?

The true center of gravity is the intersection of the lines of gravity for the vertical and horizontal orientations of the body. Imagine your body divided perfectly in half vertically and again horizontally according to weight. The intersection of the vertical and horizontal dividing lines is your center of gravity.

The center of gravity indicates the point at which weight acts regardless of the body's orientation relative to the ground. In simple terms, it is the point on which you would balance, if it were possible to balance a rigid human body on a single point.

The most interesting aspect of the center of gravity is that it constantly moves, relative to the body, as the parts of the body change position in space. Your center of gravity when you are standing, sitting and bending over are all different. In fact, your center of gravity can even move out of your body all together.

Consider a hollow object like a hoop or helmet. The centers of gravity for both are found outside their actual physical being, lying somewhere in the empty space within them. This phenomena occurs in humans too. In cases of extreme hip or trunk flexion or extension, as in some gymnastics movements, the center of gravity is found in the space that the body surrounds.

The center of gravity is important in finding equilibrium in movement and at rest. The horizontal and vertical relationships of your center of gravity to your base or stance determines the stability of your body. First, *stability is inversely proportional to the distance of the body's center of gravity to its base*. Simply stated, the closer your center of gravity is to your base, the more stable your stance is. By bending your knees and standing lower, you increase your stability. Keep in mind that this also works to the opposite effect; the lower you stand, the more you reduce your mobility.

This principle is tempered by a second principle which states that *when the center of gravity is moved to the limits of the base, only a small amount of force is necessary to upset its equilibrium*. This means that if you lean toward to the forward limits of your stance, a small amount of force can knock you over to the front. If you lean to the backward limits of your stance, a small amount of force can knock you over backwards. By placing your center of gravity in the center of your base, you form the most stable stance.

HOW DOES IT APPLY TO MARTIAL ARTS?

Balance in the martial arts is primarily derived from stable stances and reliable footwork. Some styles favor low, wide stances to increase stability. Others prefer upright, unbalanced stances to improve mobility. Depending on your style, develop what works for you. Keep in mind that mobility is increased by raising the center of gravity and placing it to the forward or backward limits of the base. Stability is increased by lowering the center of gravity and placing it in the center of the base.

Balance in movement follows a similar theory. When moving forward, shift your center of gravity forward. When moving backward, shift your center of gravity backward. This sounds obvious, but many fighters slow their movement by leaning their upper body back when they move forward or by straightening their legs and hips when they move backward.

Balance in movement is also enhanced by reducing the amount of commitment in your movements and stances. By not planting your feet in deep stances or by quickly retreating from attacks, you retain your ability to shift your balance rapidly through your movements. The key here is to control the entire movement by maintaining your center of gravity at all times. Proper balance in motion makes movement more economical and therefore faster.

HOW TO IMPROVE

Correct head placement and eye direction leads to correct body alignment. Correct body alignment is the key to static balance. If you are standing on flat ground and are not being acted on by a force other than gravity, proper body alignment allows you to stand perfectly balanced.

When moving, pay attention to details. Avoid crossing your legs. Keep your knees slightly bent during movement and landing. Take small, quick steps rather than long strides.

When a contradictory force, such as an opponent, is working against you, your center of gravity comes into play. By using a proper stance - not too wide, knees slightly bent, and center of gravity in the center or shifted slightly forward - you can resist the efforts of that force to imbalance you.

When the force unbalancing you is your motion, look for stabilizing points in the movement. Try putting less speed or power and focus on refining the execution. Once you can execute slowly with balance, increase your speed and power again.

One of the most difficult times for martial artists to maintain equilibrium is during spinning movements. During a series of spinning movements, try spotting like skaters and dancers do. Before beginning a 360 degree turn, focus on a spot in front of you. Begin your turn with your body first and at about the 180 degree point, quickly snap your head around to the front and refocus on the spot while your body completes the turn. Spotting reduces dizziness and helps you maintain a sense of continuum in motion.

Try to see your body as an interlocking whole rather than a series of moving parts that are attached. Most balance problems can be solved through slow practice with attention to your body position and alignment throughout the movement.

6-1 Head Stand   i p g

Correct execution: 1. Kneel and place your palms and head on the floor.
2. Raise your knees off the ground and extend your legs toward the ceiling.

Variation: **6-1A** If you have difficulty completing the head stand, have a
partner support your legs.

Main benefit: Improves static balance

Also improves: coordination, agility

Martial arts applications: Improves static balance in a spatially disoriented
position such as you might encounter during grappling and ground fighting.

Cautions: Falling over backwards during a head stand could result in neck
and spine injuries. Use a support until you perfect this exercise.

1. START: Hands and head on the floor.   2. Lift your body to the head stand.

6-2 Hand Stand   i p g

Correct execution: Place your palms flat on the ground and raise your legs up toward the ceiling.

Variation: **6-2A** If you cannot balance, have a partner catch and hold your legs or use a wall for support.

Main benefit: Improves static balance

Also improves: coordination, power, agility

Martial arts applications: Strengthens your ability to make the minute adjustments in body position necessary to maintain your balance.   These adjustments take place constantly during the transitions between movements and when landing.

Cautions: Falling over backwards during a handstand could result in serious neck and spine injuries. Always use a spotter or support.

Hand stand alone (6-2)

6-3 Walking on the hands   i p g

Correct execution: From a handstand position, "walk" forward by moving one hand at a time.

Variation: **6-3A** If you have trouble balancing, have a partner support your legs.

Main benefit: Improves balance in movement

Also improves: strength, ability, coordination

Martial arts applications: Upper body balance and coordination strengthen falling and throwing skills.

Cautions: Falling over backwards during a handstand could result in serious neck and spine injuries. Always use a spotter or support.

Walking on the hands

6-4 Twister p g e

Correct execution: 1. Partners face each other and hold a stick perpendicular to the ground. 2. Both partners try to turn the stick to ninety degrees, one to the left and one to the right. 3. The first to turn it in his direction wins.

Main benefit: Improves static balance

Also improves: strength

Martial arts applications: Exerting force while maintaining good balance strengthens grappling and throwing skills.

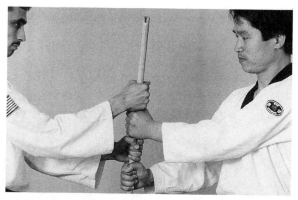

1. START: Partners grasp a stick.

2. The first to turn it to parallel wins.

6-5 Pushing kicks   p g

Correct execution: Partners stand facing each other in fighting stance. Each partner raises his right leg to a side kick position and places the sole of his foot touching the sole of his partner's foot. On cue, both people attempt to unbalance each other by pushing with their kicking leg.

Variations: **6-5A** Same exercise done with front kick
                    6-5B In the same position, hook feet and pull the other
                    person toward you

Main benefit: Improves balance on one leg

Martial arts applications: Improves balance during kicking

Pushing side kicks (6-5)

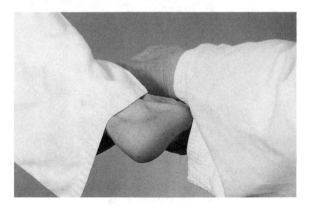

Pulling side kicks (6-5B)

6-6 Slow kicking   i p g e

Correct execution: Stand on one leg and slowly execute a kick at about waist level. Keep an even speed and concentrate on correct execution.

Variations: **6-6A** If you cannot balance alone, hold a bar or wall for support.
6-6B Face a partner and hold hands to help each other balance.

Main benefit: Improves the integration of static and dynamic balance.

Also improves: strength, coordination

Martial arts applications: By slowly executing each kick, you improve your balance throughout the technique. When you speed up, your muscles "remember" the feeling of the kick that was executed correctly with good balance.

6-7 Single Leg Balance   i g

Correct execution: Balance on one leg while moving the other leg in circles or "figure eights."

Variation: **6-7A** Close your eyes during the exercise

Main benefit: Improves static balance

Also improves: strength

Martial arts applications: Improves single leg stances and balance during kicking.

6-8 Single Leg Stretch

Correct execution: 1. Stand on your left leg and raise your right leg behind you. 2. Grasp your right foot with your right hand and pull it up and toward you while lowering your upper body. Concentrate on slow moving balance.

Variation: **6-8A** Hold a bar or wall for support if necessary

Main benefit: Improves static balance

Also improves: flexibility

Martial arts applications: This exercise helps you locate and focus on your center of gravity, improving your overall upright balance.

Single leg stretch

6-9 Single Leg Squat   i g

Correct execution: Stand on one leg and squat, holding your other leg straight out in front of you.

Main benefit: Improves balance in movement

Also improves: strength, coordination

Martial arts applications: Improves kicking by balancing on one leg while the muscles of the other leg are exerting force.

Cautions: Stop this exercise if you experience knee pain.

1. START: Stand on one leg
with the other out stretched.

2. Squat, keeping your leg straight.

6-10 Single Leg Hop   i g

Correct execution: Standing on one foot, hop as far or as long as you can.

Variation: **6-10A** Race against a partner across the room or gym

Main benefit: Improves balance in movement

Also improves: strength, coordination

Martial arts applications: Improves kicking and footwork, especially single leg penetration attacks (i.e. sliding in side kick).

Single leg hop

6-11 Windmill   i g

Correct execution: 1. Stand with your right leg about eighteen inches behind your left. 2. Bend forward and touch your right hand to your right foot.

Main benefit: Improves static balance

Also improves: flexibility

Martial arts applications: Improves balance when a proper stance cannot be achieved.

1. Stand with your right leg behind your left. 2. Touch your right hand to right foot.

6-12 Back to back stand   p g

Correct execution: 1. Partners sit back to back. 2. On cue, both stand up simultaneously, while maintaining contact. 3. Once standing, they squat simultaneously, again maintaining contact.

Main benefit: Improves balance in movement

Also improves: perception, coordination

Martial arts applications: Improves balance and cooperation when working with or against another person, as in grappling and throwing arts.

1. START: Partners sit back to back.   2. Partners stand while keeping in contact.

6-13 Seated pull-ups   p g

Correct execution: 1. Partners sit with their legs extended, feet touching and hands clasped. 2. On cue, they pull each towards each other and raise their buttocks off the floor.

Main benefit: Improves balance in movement

Also improves: strength, agility, flexibility

Martial arts applications: Balancing with a partner heightens your sensitivity to other's balance and weight shifts. Good for increasing balance in grappling, throwing and takedowns.

6-14 Gombae Paree   p g

Correct execution: Partners face each other and hold one of their feet with both hands. When the referee says go, each tries to knock the other down, using only his body weight. The first to fall is the loser. If either person drops his leg or uses his hands to push or grab the partner, he is the loser.

Variation: **6-14A** For added challenge try two on one or two on two.

Main benefit: Improves balance in movement

Also improves: coordination, strength, endurance

Martial arts applications: Improves body weight shifting and balance for kicking and footwork.

Cautions: Pair even size partners and do not allow horseplay.

1. Stand on one leg, holding the other   2. Partners try to knock each other down

6-15 Partner Bridge   p g

Correct execution: Partners stand facing each other and place their hands on each other's shoulders. Each person takes one step back. They continue to take single steps backward until they can no longer balance.

Main benefit: Improves balance while external pressure is being applied.

Also improves: strength, endurance, flexibility

Martial arts applications: Strengthens resistance to the opponent's pressure in throwing and takedown applications.

Cautions: Discontinue this exercise if you have shoulder pain or an existing shoulder injury.

Partners move as far from each other as possible without falling.

6-16 Horse Stance drill   p g

Correct execution: Partners face each other in horse riding stance. They place their palms together and on cue try to push each other over backwards.

Variations: **6-16A** Also can be done in front or back stance
                     6-16B Partners grasp hands and try to pull each other
                     forwards off balance in any of the above stances.

Main benefit: Improves balance while external pressure is being applied

Martial arts applications: Strengthens resistance to the opponents attacks in throwing and striking applications.

Cautions: Pair even size partners and do not allow horseplay.

Horse stance, pushing hands. (6-16)

Horse stance pulling hands (6-16B)

6-17 Tug of War   p g

Correct execution: Partners face each other and hold opposite ends of a belt. On cue, they both pull toward themselves, trying to unbalance the opponent.

Variations: **6-17A** If there are many students, divide them into teams, using shorts ropes instead of belts.
6-17B Using a rope tied into a circle, form a circle and have everyone pull toward themselves

Main benefit: Improves static balance

Also improves: strength

Martial arts applications: Strengthens stances

Cautions: Pair even size partners and watch out for collisions if one partner suddenly gives up. When using a rope, use proper hand protection to prevent rope burn.

TRACKING YOUR PROGRESS

The following exercises will help you track your progress. For balance exercises, count only each successful repetition. A successful repetition is one that you complete without any balance faults like touching your support or dropping your leg.

1. Single leg squat (# 6-9)

DATE	REPETITIONS	DATE	REPETITIONS

TRACKING YOUR PROGRESS

2. Single leg hop (# 6-10)

Mark off a distance on the floor and try to hop without falling or dropping your other leg. Count only the distance you can hop without errors. Record your best distance.

DATE	DISTANCE	DATE	DISTANCE

INSTRUCTOR'S NOTES

① Balance exercises are essential for arts that stress kicking and/or throwing and takedown skills. Almost all of these skills require excellent balance, both in motion and at rest.

② Some students will have difficulty with balance because of inner ear problems. These problems cannot be fixed through exercise, though you may see some improvement over time. If you sense a student has a physical impediment to balance, do not place too much stress on this aspect of training for him or her.

③ Installing bars along the walls of the training area is useful for balance practice as well as for flexibility training. A session at the bar working on a specific kick brings rapid improvement for beginners and intermediate students.

④ For beginners do all balance drills on flat, firm surfaces to prevent ankle injuries. Once students have mastered the exercises on flat surfaces, try them on firm and then soft mats for an increased challenge.

⑤ Children need a lot of balance work, especially those under the age of eight years old. Start with simple, low risk skills like walking on a straight line or two-by-four then progress to single leg drills. Watch for children who have weak knees and ankles, a common condition in developing bodies.

7

AGILITY

WHAT IS IT?

Agility is the ability to change direction or body position quickly and proceed smoothly with another movement. It is often confused with coordination. While coordination is a part of agility, true agility is something more. It is a kind of physical intelligence. Agility is the characteristic present in people who are called natural athletes. It is much more common in small or average size people than in tall or large people.

WHERE DOES IT COME FROM?

Agility is a partially innate characteristic that can be improved somewhat through practice. Identifying a single source of agility is almost impossible. Agility is an amorphous quality that is hard to pinpoint, but you always know when someone has it. It is the foundation upon which great athletes are built. Essentially, agility is a smoothly integrated combination of perception, coordination, speed, strength and balance.

HOW DOES IT APPLY TO MARTIAL ARTS?

Martial arts are based on the development of smooth combinations of movements. Forms, sparring drills, self-defense techniques and free-sparring are all examples of groups of skills that must be linked together quickly and coherently. Agility provides that link. Agility is also important in responding quickly and correctly to an opponent. Skillful evasion and footwork are based on moving swiftly and changing direction frequently in response to the opponent's actions.

HOW TO IMPROVE

Agility is a primarily inborn quality. Improvement comes slowly through experience. Using your body to its fullest potential in every movement, whether in martial arts or in other physical activities, helps you learn how your body responds to your demands. In the same way that studying strengthens your mental intelligence, seriously engaging in physical pursuits strengthens your physical intelligence. The more you use your body, the smarter it becomes.

In practice, focus on moving your body as a single unit. Mobilize your center of gravity as the core of all movements. To achieve this, imagine your body is a wheel and axle. The axle runs through the center of your body and the wheel is your limbs, which rotate around the axle. By fixing your axle, you can change direction quickly and be poised for an immediate follow-up movement.

To find and fix your axle while changing direction changes, you must have good posture. Good posture comes from a proper fighting stance. Align your head and spine and keep you arms in a relaxed guard position. Tighten your hips and bend your knees slightly. Bounce or rest lightly on your feet with your weight shifted slightly forward. From this stance, you are prepared to move or strike quickly in any direction.

By practicing movements based on the wheel and axle model, your direction changes and transitional movements will become more natural and therefore faster and more effective.

7-1 Jumping drills   i g

Correct execution: Jump and touch your knees to your chest

Variations: **7-1A** Jump and touch your feet to your buttocks
7-1B Jump and touch your feet to your hands in front of
you
7-1C Jump and touch your feet to your hands stretched
out to the side

Main benefit: Improves upper and lower body coordination

Also improves: strength, flexibility

Martial arts applications: Improves jumping kicks

Jump and touch your feet to your hands (7-1B)

Jump and touch your knees to your chest (7-1)

7-2 Zig-zag run   i   g

Correct execution: Run fifty to one hundred yards in a zig-zag pattern.

Variation: 7-2A Hop the same distance in a zig-zag pattern

Main benefit: Improves total body agility

Also improves: coordination, speed

Martial arts applications: Improves footwork and body shifting speed

7-3 Shuttle Run   i   g   e

Correct execution: Mark off two lines on the ground, ten to twenty yards apart. Start at one line and sprint to the other, touch it and come back.

Variations: 7-3A Place two small objects on each line. Instead of touching the line, pick up the object and carry it to the other line. Then place it down and pick up a different object to carry back to the first line. Complete two circuits.

7-3B Mark off four lines ten yards apart. Start on line one and run to line two. Return to line one then run to line three. Return to line one then run to line four. Return to line one.

Main benefit: Improves total body agility

Other benefits: endurance, speed

Martial arts application: Improves quickness in changing direction and body height for sparring and grappling.

Cautions: Watch for knee and ankle injuries during the touch down and turn phase of this exercise.

7-4 Backwards run   i g

Correct execution: Run fifty to one hundred yards backwards

Main benefit: Improves total body agility

Also improves: coordination, perception, balance

Martial arts applications: Improves defensive footwork

Cautions: Run on a firm surface free of obstacles to prevent falling backward.

7-5 Footwork drill   i g

Correct execution: In fighting stance, alternately slide right to left

Variation: 7-5A Alternately slide front to back

Main benefit: Improves lower body agility

Also improves: timing, speed, coordination

Martial arts applications: Improves footwork speed and mobility

7-6 Bouncing drill   i g

Correct execution: With both feet together bounce side to side.

Variation: 7-6A Bounce front to back

Main benefit: Improves body shifting and mobility

Also improves: strength, coordination, balance

Martial arts applications: Improves footwork speed and mobility as well as a sense of moving the entire body as one unit.

7-7 Shadow Sparring   i g

Correct execution: Spar with an imaginary opponent for a one to three minute round.

Main benefit: Improves total body agility

Also improves: Coordination, timing, endurance

Martial arts applications: Improves sparring skills

7-8 Shoulder Standing   i g

Correct execution: 1. Lie on your back. 2. Raise your legs toward the ceiling transferring your weight onto your upper back and shoulders and place your hands on your hips for support.

Variation: 7-8A For an added challenge, lower your legs so your feet touch the floor above your head.

Main benefit: Improves overall body agility

Also improves: flexibility, balance

Martial arts applications: Improves falling and ground skills

Cautions: Stop if you experience back or neck pain.

Stretch your feet toward the ceiling.

7-9 Spinal Roll   i g

Correct execution: 1. Sit with your knees drawn up to your chest and your hands clasped around your thighs. 2. Roll backward and extend your legs straight over your head so your feet touch the ground above your head.

Main benefit: Improves total body agility

Also improves: flexibility

Martial arts applications: Improves falling and ground skills.

Cautions: Stop if you have neck or back pain.

1. START: Sit and grasp your knees.

2. Roll backward

3. Extend your legs over your head.

7-10 Bridge   i p g

Correct execution: 1. Lie on your back with your knees bent and feet flat on the floor. 2. Place your palms on the floor next to your head and raise your body up onto your hands and feet.

Variation: 7-10A If you cannot lift your body off the floor, have a partner support your lower back and lift you gently.

Main benefit: Improves trunk agility

Also improves: balance, flexibility, strength, coordination

Martial arts applications: Strengthens the trunk muscles to improve jumping and kicking skills.

Cautions: Stop this exercise if you have back pain.

Press up, transferring your weight to your hands and feet.

7-11 Hand circles   i g

Correct execution: 1. Place one hand and both feet on the floor. 2. "Walk" as quickly as possible around the supporting arm.

Main benefit: Improves total body agility

Also improves: strength, balance

Martial arts applications: Balancing while moving quickly on the ground is important in ground fighting.

1. START: Place one hand on the floor.

2. Walk around the supporting hand.

7-12 Cartwheel   i g

Correct execution: Place your right and then your left hand on the floor while your body follows in a pinwheel motion.

Main benefit: Improves total body agility

Also improves: coordination, strength

Martial arts applications: Emphasizes the lightness in the lower body that is necessary for agile footwork and kicking.

1. Stand with arms outstretched.   2. Place your hands on the floor and let your legs follow.

7-13 Leg raises   i g

Correct execution: From a standing position, swing one leg up in front of you, then step down and repeat with the other leg.

Variations: **7-13A** Swing to the side
7-13B Swing to the rear
7-13C Swing in an arc up to the rear and then up to the front without stopping.

Main benefit: Lower body agility

Also improves: flexibility

Martial arts applications: Moving one leg while balancing on the other is essential in kicking and throwing applications.

1. Swing your leg to the front. (7-13)   2. Swing your leg to the rear. (7-13B)

Swing your leg to the side (7-13A)

7-14 Squat drill   p g

Correct execution: 1. Partners squat facing each other and holding hands. 2. Both partners extend their right leg straight out in front of them. 3. They then both switch to their left leg and continue alternating in this way.

Main benefit: Improves lower body agility

Also improves: power, speed, balance

Martial arts applications: Improves agility in kicking and footwork

Cautions: Stop this exercise if you have knee pain. Do not try this exercise if you have an existing knee injury.

Alternately thrust out your right and left legs.

7-15 Turn around wrestling   p g

Correct execution: 1. Partners sit back to back. 2. On command each turns around to a kneeling position and grips the other's shoulders or arms. 3. The first to make the other touch any part of his body to the ground is the winner.

Main benefit: Improves total body agility

Also improves: balance, speed, strength

Martial arts benefit: Improves positioning, stance, gripping and strategy for grappling.

1. START: Partners sit back to back.

2. On cue, turn and engage.

TRACKING YOUR PROGRESS

Tracking your progress in agility exercises can only be done through your observation of the increasing skill with which you complete each drill or exercise. For example, as you practice the footwork drill you will find that it becomes easier to transfer your body weight and you can move more quickly. Use this page to make notes regarding your observations of improvement in the drills and exercises you use.

INSTRUCTOR'S NOTES

① Agility is a vague quality, especially in the minds of beginners. Trying consciously to improve agility may lead beginners to frustration. Use these exercises in class, but do not overemphasize the necessity of developing agility. Through these exercises, students will develop a general feeling of increased body confidence and overall fitness.

② Drills like footwork, bouncing and running are good for starting class. They serve the dual purpose of preparing the body for exercise and improving total body coordination.

③ Skills that require coordinated body movement such as throwing, falling, kicking and jumping benefit from specific skill practice as well as general agility training.

8

FLEXIBILITY

WHAT IS IT?

Flexibility is the extent to which a joint can be moved through its normal range of motion. It is primarily related to the elasticity of the adjoining muscles and their fascia (sheaths). If the muscles and their surrounding tissues are highly elastic, the joint is able to move through its maximum range of motion. If the muscles are tight, the range of motion is limited.

Although muscles are generally long enough to accommodate the full range of motion, they are limited in elasticity by the conditioned response of the myotatic reflex.

WHERE DOES IT COME FROM?

In addition to muscle elasticity, flexibility is affected by the tightness of the ligaments attached to the joint and the strength of the muscles. Ligaments require a certain amount of tension to firmly support the joint. While a ligament that is too tight limits the range of motion, a ligament that is overstretched creates instability in the joint.

Muscle strength should be developed with flexibility. Muscles that are lacking in strength, tend to overstretch, leading to joint and ligament injuries. By developing a balance of strength and flexibility, you create muscles that can withstand tension while working through their entire range of motion.

HOW DOES IT APPLY TO MARTIAL ARTS?

Good flexibility promotes smooth, efficient, light movements. Since many martial arts movements are evaluated on the look and feel of their execution, as in forms, smooth movements are highly desirable. Flexibility is also necessary for high kicks, jumping, acrobatic skills and deep stances.

More fundamentally, flexibility encourages the proper use of natural body mechanics by removing any hindrance to large movements. It allows you to make a full range of motion which is the key to making maximum speed and power.

To make maximum power, muscles should first lengthen fully, then contract fully. If your muscles are short, your potential to create force is limited. Imagine a baseball pitcher. He elongates his arm and upper body in his windup, then contracts in his delivery. Similar examples can be found in martial arts, such as a hip throw. The thrower opens his hips, chest and shoulders, then contracts them to throw.

HOW TO IMPROVE

Stretch every time you exercise. The only way to improve your flexibility is through consistent stretching exercises. Every muscle is subject to the myotatic reflex (stretch reflex) which opposes changes in muscle length, especially sudden or extreme changes. When a muscle lengthens beyond a certain point, the myotatic reflex causes it to tighten and attempt to shorten. This is the tension you feel during stretching exercises.

The myotatic reflex is desirable because it prevents, in many cases, muscle strains and tears. Without it your muscles would be allowed to overextend and tear easily. But it is also undesirable in cases where it prevents you from fully using your body.

Through stretching, deconditioning of the myotatic reflex takes place. Little by little, you teach your muscles a new limit of safe extension. This is why stretching must be slow and consistent. If you overstretch and injure the muscle, you have to go back to a lower level of flexibility and start over. Set your stretching goals over a period of weeks or months, not days, for best results.

There are three types of stretching: static, dynamic and ballistic. **Ballistic stretching** means bobbing, bouncing or using some type of moving pressure to stretch the target muscles. Ballistic stretching is not recommended because it activates the myotatic reflex and causes the muscles to tense, rather than relax. Ballistic stretching has a high risk of injury.

Dynamic stretching means moving the muscle through its full range of movement. Dynamic stretching leads to greater flexibility in movement but should be done with caution so it does not become ballistic stretching. To maintain a correct dynamic stretch, focus on smooth, even movements that do not shock the muscle. Examples of dynamic stretches are knee raises, leg raises, arm circles, and trunk circles.

Static stretching is a controlled stretch. A specific muscle or muscle group is extended to the point of feeling slight pain and held in that position for ten to sixty seconds. During static stretching, concentrate on relaxing the target muscles and breathing deeply.

Begin your flexibility workout with several minutes of gross motor activity to increase your blood flow. Increased blood flow improves the suppleness of the muscles. Then move to joint loosening exercises followed by dynamic stretches to the get the muscles moving freely. If you are working only on flexibility, do static stretches next. If you are training, interspersing periods of static stretching throughout the workout works best because the range of motion increases as the body warms up. Do some light static stretches at the end of every workout to relax and refresh your muscles.

CAUTIONS

❖ Do not overstretch. A mild sensation of burning or pulling should be felt in the target muscles. It should be uncomfortable but not unbearable.

❖ Avoid bouncing during a stretch. Bouncing causes the muscles to tighten and heightens the risk of injury.

❖ Follow instructions for exercises carefully. There is right and wrong way to stretch every muscle. Good flexibility exercises are designed to provide a maximum stretch with a minimum risk of injury.

❖ Do gravity assisted stretches with caution and only after fully warming up. Gravity assisted stretches are exercises like splits that use the force of gravity to increase the pressure on the stretch.

❖ You should never feel pain in your joints during stretching exercises. If you do, stop immediately and discontinue that exercise.

❖ When doing flexibility exercises that require bending at the waist, always bend from the hip, not the lower back. The lower back is extremely vulnerable to injuries.

❖ Always increase strength and flexibility together.

EXERCISES

The flexibility exercises in this chapter have been divided into three groups:
       1. Neck, shoulders and arms (8-1 to 8-12)
       2. Chest, abdomen and back (8-13 to 8-24)
       3. Buttocks and legs (8-25 to 8-39)

8-1 Neck rotation   i g

Correct execution: Beginning at the right shoulder, slowly rotate the head across the chest and to the left shoulder then back.

Variations: **8-1A** Look to the left and to the right alternately
8-1B Look up and down alternately.

Main benefit: Prepares neck muscles for exercise

Martial arts applications: Prevents neck injuries in falling exercises and increases flexibility for spotting during turning.

Cautions: Never rotate the head to the rear because it puts undesirable pressure on the vertebrae. Always perform slowly.

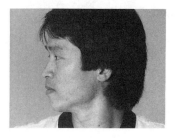

1. Begin at the right shoulder.

2. Slowly rotate to the left. (8-1)

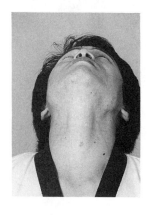

1. Look up . . .

2. then down. (8-1B)

8-2 Arm circles   i g

Correct execution: 1. Stretch both arms out to the side. 2. Rotate them in large circles to the front

Variations: **8-2A** Rotate in large circles to the rear
                    8-2B Rotate in small circles to the front
                    8-2C Rotate in small circles to the rear

Main benefit: Stretches shoulders

Martial arts applications: Improves circular striking and throwing

Rotate in large circles (8-2)

Rotate in small circles (8-2B)

8-3 Press, press, fling   i g

Correct execution: 1. Stand with your arms outstretched in front of you. 2. Thrust your elbows to the rear two times. 3. Swing your arms to the rear once. Return to the start position after each movement.

Main benefit: Stretches shoulders and chest

Martial arts applications: Good warm-up for striking and throwing

1. START: Stand with arms extended.   2. Thrust elbows to rear twice.

3. Swing your arms to the rear.

8-4 Half windmills   i g

Correct execution: 1. Stretch one arm over your head and let the other hang at your side. 2. Simultaneously thrust both arms to the rear twice. 3. Switch arms and repeat.

Main benefit: Stretches shoulders and chest

Martial arts applications: Improves flexibility for striking and throwing skills that require moving both arms in different directions.

1. Right arm up and left arm down.   2. Thrust to the rear.

8-5 Arm raises   i g

Correct execution: 1. Stand with your feet a bit more than shoulder width apart and your fists touching the ground. 2. Extend your right arm up above your back while keeping your left fist on the ground. Alternate.

Main benefit: Stretches shoulders

Martial arts applications: Improves flexibility for throwing and striking skills.

1. Feet apart and fists on the ground.   2. Alternately thrust your arms upward.

8-6 Shoulder stretch   i g

Correct execution: 1. Raise your right arm above your head and bend at the elbow. 2. Press down on your elbow with your left hand. 3. Grasp your right hand and pull to the left with your left hand. 4. Put your right hand over your left shoulder and press your right elbow with your left hand.

Main benefit: Stretches shoulder

Martial arts applications: Reduces the risk of shoulder injury in locking and falling applications.

1. Raise your arm and bend at the elbow.

2. Grasp your hand and pull.

3. Put your hand over your shoulder and push.

8-7 Rear arm stretch   i g

Correct execution: 1. Stretch both arms behind your back and interlock your fingers with your thumbs pointing to the ground. 2. Raise your arms toward the ceiling.

Main benefit: Stretch shoulders

Martial arts applications: Improves flexibility for striking and throwing

Cautions: Do not do this exercise if you have a previous shoulder injury, especially a shoulder dislocation.

Interlock your fingers behind your back and raise your arms.

8-8 Inside forearm stretch   i g

Correct execution: Grasp the fingers of your right hand with your left hand and pull towards you (right palm facing away from you).

Main benefit: Stretches forearm, wrist and fingers

Martial arts applications: Good warm-up for joint locking and snapping strikes like backfist

Inside forearm stretch (8-8)

8-9 Outside forearm stretch   i g

Correct execution: Grasp your right hand with your left hand and press towards your right elbow.

Main benefit: Stretches forearm, wrist and fingers

Martial arts applications: Good warm-up for joint locking practice

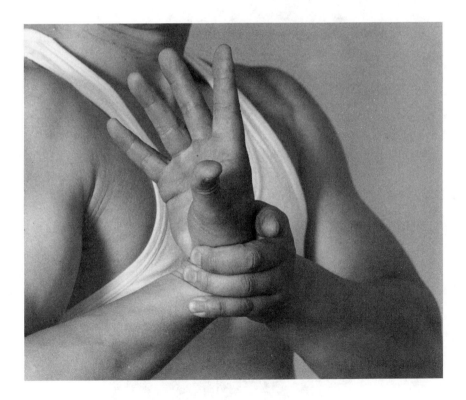

Outside forearm stretch (8-9)

8-10 Wrist flex   i g

Correct execution: 1. Grasp your right hand with your left hand. 2. Pull toward your chest. 3. Push away from your body.

Main benefit: Stretches wrist

Martial arts applications: Good warm-up for joint locking, striking and weapons practice

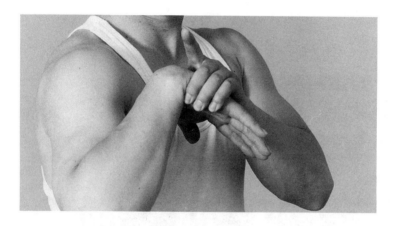

1. Flex your wrist and pull toward you.

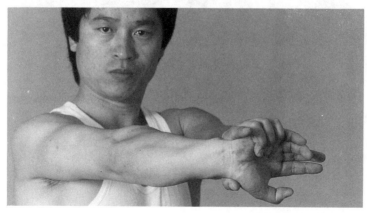

2. Flex your wrist away from you.

8-11 Finger press   i g

Correct execution: 1. Stretch your arms in front of you and interlock your fingers with your thumbs facing downward. 2. Stretch and flex your elbows.

Main benefit: Stretches fingers and wrist

Martial arts applications: Improves strength and flexibility for grabbing applications.

1. Interlock your fingers and stretch outward.

2. Flex toward your chest.

8-12 Trunk twist

i g

Correct execution: 1. Stand with your feet a bit more than shoulder width apart and your arms stretched out to the side. 2. Bend forward at the waist and alternately touch your toes with your outstretched arms.

Main benefit: Stretches upper back and shoulders

Martial arts applications: Improves agility in falling and throwing skills.

1. START: Stand with your arms outstretched and feet apart.

2. Stretch to alternately touch your toes.

8-13 Trunk bend   i g

Correct execution: 1. Stand with both feet shoulder width apart and arms outstretched. 2. Bend forward and touch the ground in front of you. 3. Reach through your legs and touch the ground behind you. 4. Stand up and lean back, opening your arms wide.

Main benefit: Stretches chest and back

Martial arts applications: Increases the range of trunk movement in throwing and takedowns.

1. Stand with arms outstretched.

2. Bend and touch the ground in front.

2. Touch the ground behind.

3. Bend backward.

8-14 Chest opening   i g

Correct execution: 1. Lie on your stomach with your hands in push-up position. 2. Push your chest and upper abdomen off the ground and fully extend your arms while looking upward.

Main benefit: Stretches chest and abdomen

Martial arts applications: Improves flexibility for throwing and striking skills.

1. START: Lie on your stomach.

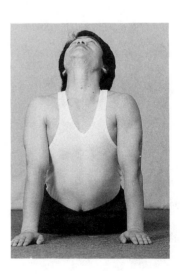

2. Lift your body and look upward.

8-15 Inverse chest opening   i g

Correct execution: 1. Sit with your hands behind you and palms on the floor. 2. Lift your torso, shifting your weight onto your feet and hands while looking behind you.

Variation: **8-15A** Alternately raise your legs off the floor

Main benefit: Stretches chest and shoulders

Also improves: arm strength

Martial arts applications: Improves flexibility for throwing and striking.

Lean back and lift your lower body off the floor.

8-16 Seated trunk twist   i g

Correct execution: 1. Sit with your left leg crossed over your right leg.
2. Put your right arm on your left leg and turn to your right. Alternate sides.

Main benefit: Improves trunk flexibility

Martial arts applications: Improves flexibility for striking, throwing and
spinning skills.

Seated trunk twist (8-16)

8-17 Lying trunk twist   i g

Correct execution: 1. Lie on your back with both arms outstretched to the side. 2. Raise your right knee and twist your body to touch your knee to the floor on your left side. Alternate sides.

Variations: **8-17A**   Raise your leg straight up and touch your foot to your opposite hand.
8-17B   Lie on your stomach in the same position and touch your foot to your opposite hand.

Main benefit: Improves trunk flexibility

Martial arts applications: Improves flexibility for kicking and spinning.

With your leg straight (8-17A)

Lying on your stomach (8-17B)

8-18 Side bends i g

Correct execution: Standing, raise one arm and stretch it over your head while you bend to the side.

Main benefit: Stretches side (oblique) muscles

Martial arts applications: Improves flexibility for throwing and striking

1. START: Stretch one arm upward.   2. Bend to the side.

8-19 Back stretch   i g

Correct execution: Kneel and lean forward with your upper body, stretching your arms above your head.

Main benefit: Stretches back

Martial arts applications: Improves flexibility for kicking, striking and throwing skills.

Kneel and reach forward.

8-20 Back roll   i g

Correct execution: 1. Sit with your knees bent and your hands clasped around your thighs. 2. Gently roll back until your shoulder blades touch the floor and then roll up to the starting position.

Main benefit: Stretches back

Martial arts applications: Strengthens and loosens the spine for falling and throwing.

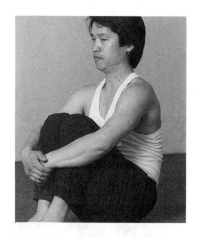

1. START: Sit with your hands clasped around your knees.

2. Gently roll back.

8-21 Criss cross   i g

Correct execution: 1. Stretch both arms in front of you. 2. Cross your arms right over left, left over right, right over left, then thrust both arms to the rear.

Main benefit: Stretches chest and back

Martial arts applications: Good warm-up for striking and throwing

1. START: Stretch your arms in front.   2. Alternately cross them 3 times.

3. Thrust both arms to the rear.

8-22 Up-back-over   i g

Correct execution: 1. Swing your arms up. 2. Swing your arms down to the rear. 3. Swing your arms over your head in a circle to the rear.

Main benefit: Stretches chest and back

Martial arts applications: Improves throwing and takedown skills that move both arms together.

1. Swing your arms up.

2. Swing your arms down.

3. Circle your arms over your head.

8-23 Back lift   p g

Correct execution: 1. Stand back to back with a partner and lock your arms at the elbow. 2. One partner leans forward, lifting the other onto his back.

Main benefit: Stretches back and chest

Also improves: strength, balance

Martial arts applications: Improves flexibility for throwing and kicking skills.

Cautions: Always do this exercise with a partner of similar weight and height. Load the person slowly onto your back. Do not do this exercise if you have back or knee injuries.

1. Stand back to back and lock arms.   2. Bend and lift your partner.

8-24 Partner trunk twist   p g

Correct execution: 1. Stand back to back with a partner. 2. Both partners twist their upper body to the right and touch palms. Alternate sides.

Variation: **8-24A** One partner twists to the left while the other twists to the right. Alternate

Main benefit: Increases trunk flexibility

Also improves: coordination

Martial arts applications: Improves spinning and throwing skills.

1. START: Stand back to back.   2. Twist to the right and touch hands.

8-25 Hip rotation   i g

Correct execution: Place your hands on your hips and rotate your hips clockwise. Reverse and rotate counterclockwise.

Main benefit: Improves hip flexibility

Martial arts applications: Improves kicking height and range of motion.

Place your hands on your hips and rotate your hips.

8-26 Knee rotation   i g

Correct execution: 1. Stand with both knees together. 2. Place your hands on your knees and rotate them clockwise. Reverse and rotate counter clockwise.

Main benefit: Increases knee flexibility

Martial arts applications: Good warm-up for footwork and kicking

Place your hands on your knees and rotate.

8-27 Toe touch   i g

Correct execution: 1. Stand with both feet together and knees straight. 2. Bend at the waist and touch your toes with your hands.

Variations: **8-27A** Palms to the floor
8-27B Cross your legs and touch your toes
8-27C Begin in a squat with both palms on the floor and stand up as far as you can while maintaining your hand position.

Main benefit: Improves back, buttock and hamstring flexibility

Martial arts applications: Improves kicking height and stance depth.

Touch your toes (8-27)

Palms to floor (8-27A)

Legs crossed (8-27B)

8-28 Groin stretch   i g

Correct execution: 1. Stand with your feet about twice your shoulder width apart. 2. Squat to the side with one leg bent and the other extended to the side. Alternate sides.

Main benefit: Stretches groin and thigh muscles

Martial arts applications: Improves kicking height and range

Groin stretch (8-28)

8-29 Knee raises   i p g

Correct execution: 1. Stand with your feet shoulder width apart. 2. Raise one knee up as high as you can. Alternate sides.

Variations: **8-29A** Twist to touch your knee to the opposite elbow
8-29B Lean your back against a wall and have a partner push your knee up to your chest and hold it.
8-29C Rotate the leg outward ninety degrees to open the hip

Main benefit: Stretches hips and hamstrings

Martial arts applications: Improves kicking height, range and speed.

Knee raise (8-29)

Knee raise and twist (8-29A)

Knee raise with a partner (8-29B)

Knee raise and open (8-29C)

8-30 Partner leg raises   p g

Correct execution: Standing, have your partner raise one leg up in front of you without bending your knee.

Variations: **8-30A** Side leg raises
                   8-30B Rear leg raises

Main benefit: Stretches hips and legs

Also improves: strength

Martial arts applications: Improves kicking height and range.

Cautions: The stretching partner should indicate when to stop raising the leg to avoid overstretching.

Leg raise to the front (8-30)   Leg raise to the side (8-30B)

8-31 Butterfly stretch   i g

Correct execution: 1. Sit with your knees bent and soles of the feet touching. 2. Lean forward with your upper body while applying pressure to your knees with your arms.

Main benefit: Stretches hips and inner thighs

Martial arts applications: Improves kicking range.

Cautions: Do not allow anyone to stand on or put their full body weight on your legs during this exercise.

Butterfly stretch (8-31)

8-32 Knee pull   i g

Correct execution: Seated, bend your knee and pull it to your chest with both arms.

Main benefit: Stretches hips, hamstrings and buttocks

Martial arts applications: Improves kicking range

Seated, pull your leg toward you

8-33 Leg extension   i g

Correct execution: Seated, grasp the arch of your foot and pull your foot toward you, keeping your knee straight.

Variation: **8-33A** Can also be done lying on your back.

Main benefit: Stretches hamstrings and buttocks

Martial arts applications: Improves kicking height

1. Seated grasp the arch of your foot.

2. Straighten your leg. (8-33)

1. Lying back, grasp the arch of your foot.

2. Straighten your leg. (8-33A)

8-34 Double quadriceps stretch   i g

Correct execution: Kneel, then lie back with your legs folded under you.

Main benefit: Stretches quadriceps (thigh) muscles

Martial arts applications: Improves kicking initiation speed and flexibility.

Cautions: Stop if you have knee pain.

1. Kneel.

2. Lie back with your knees bent.

8-35 Hurdler stretch   i g

Correct execution: 1. Sit with one leg bent to the side and one extended in front of you. 2. Stretch forward to touch your opposite side toes. 3. Lie back and stretch your thigh muscles. Alternate sides.

Main benefit: Stretches muscles in the front and back of the thighs

Martial arts applications: Improves kicking height and speed.

Cautions: Stop if you have knee pain.

1. Stretch forward.

2. Stretch backward.

8-36 Splits   i g

Correct execution: Extend one leg in front of and one leg behind your body, keeping your knees straight.

Variations: **8-36A** If you cannot reach the floor, bend your rear leg and put your rear knee on the floor for support.
8-36B Center split: Extend one leg out to each side and support yourself on your hands.

Main benefit: Stretches hips and legs

Martial arts applications: Improves kicking height and range

Side split (8-37)

Center split (8-37B)

8-37 Straddle stretch   i p g

Correct execution: 1. Seated, spread your legs to the sides. 2. Bend at the waist and stretch forward, then to the right foot, then to the left foot.

Variation: **8-37A** Sit facing a partner in the starting position with your feet touching. Grasp hands. One partner lies back while the other leans forward. Alternate positions.

Main benefit: Stretches legs and hips

Martial arts applications: Improves kicking height

Cautions: During the partner stretch, the partner leaning forward should indicate if the stretch is painful.

1. Bend to the side.

2. Bend to the center.

8-38 Seated toe touch   i p g

Correct execution: 1. Sit with your legs extended in front of you and together, with your knees straight. 2. Raise your arms above your head and bend at the waist to touch your hands to your toes.

Variation: **8-38A** Facing a partner, sit in the starting position with the soles of your feet touching. Grasp hands. One partner leans back while the other partner leans forward.

Main benefit: Stretches hamstrings

Martial arts applications: Improves kicking height

Cautions: During the partner stretch, the partner leaning forward should indicate if the stretch is painful.

Seated toe touch (8-38)

8-39 Ankle rotation   i g

Correct execution: 1. Sit with your right leg outstretched and your left leg resting on it. 2. Grasp your left foot with your right hand and gently rotate it to the right and then to the left.

Main benefit: Loosens ankle joint

Martial arts applications: Good warm-up for footwork and jumping drills.

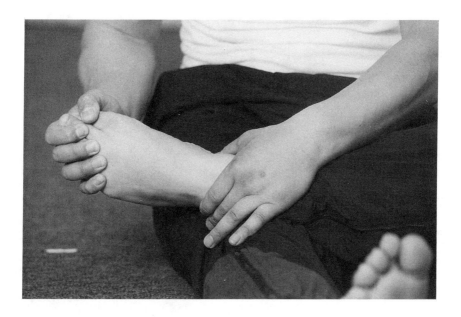

Rotate your ankle

TRACKING YOUR PROGRESS

Tracking your progress in flexibility training is possible by measuring your maximum stretch. However, this can lead you to overstretch just to get a better reading for your records. Instead, concentrate on how you feel during your stretching and during your training.

Increased flexibility directly results in improved performance. You feel the results of your effort in every movement. Measure your flexibility not in numbers, but in the enjoyment you feel when you kick higher, twist farther, spin more, and strike through your entire range of motion.

INSTRUCTOR'S NOTES

① A lack of flexibility is the number one complaint among adult students. Spend at least ten to fifteen minutes of every adult beginner class for flexibility exercises.

② Children who have not yet reached puberty have almost limitless flexibility. There is little need to spend time for flexibility exercises for them. Caution them against over stretching because their joints are often unstable.

③ When children reach puberty and especially during the growth spurts that characterize adolescence, they undergo a period of tightness in their muscles. This is the time when their bones are growing rapidly and their muscles and ligaments are struggling to catch up. Prescribe an individual daily stretching regimen for these youngsters. This is a frustrating period and they need special guidance to overcome its challenges.

④ Begin every class with a warm-up followed by a full stretch. At the end of class, cool down by repeating some key stretching exercises. Many students find an increase in flexibility at the end of class when their muscles are warm and active.

9

ENDURANCE

WHAT IS IT?

There are two types of endurance. The most common interpretation of endurance is cardiovascular endurance, which is the ability of the heart, lungs and vascular system to function efficiently for an extended period of time.

Muscular endurance, the other type, is the ability of muscles or muscle groups to sustain repeated contractions over time. Muscular endurance is important for strength and mechanically correct movement. When muscular endurance is high, the muscles produce more force than when endurance is poor. The body also functions more efficiently when endurance is high, because the muscles are able to execute movements repeatedly without tiring.

WHERE DOES IT COME FROM?

Aerobic energy

Aerobic energy, the type most closely related to cardiovascular endurance training, is literally energy derived from oxygen. Aerobic energy is the energy that your body uses during prolonged activity. It is derived primarily from the metabolism of carbohydrates and fats in the presence of oxygen.

Aerobic energy production relies on three components:
1. The lungs' efficiency in exchanging oxygen for carbon dioxide
2. The heart's ability to pump sufficient amounts of blood at an adequate rate
3. The vascular system's ability to provide the muscles with an adequate supply of oxygen-rich blood

Aerobic capacity is increased through exercising the aerobic energy production system. Through consistent aerobic exercise, the heart pumps more efficiently and blood volume increases to create a greater supply of oxygen to the muscles. When aerobic exercise is discontinued, the cardiovascular system begins to decrease in efficiency in a few weeks.

Anaerobic Energy

Anaerobic energy is created without oxygen. It is derived from phosphates and stored glycogen and can only be produced in small amounts. It is the type of energy you use for short, intense bursts of activity.

Anaerobic energy is not often associated with endurance activities. Most endurance building activities focus on strengthening the aerobic energy production system through lengthy workouts like running, biking and swimming. Anaerobic energy is important for endurance in sports like basketball and football where short bursts of energy are required many times over a period of hours. Relying on only aerobic energy production, athletes in these sports would not be able to make fast breaks or run eighty yards for a touchdown.

HOW DOES IT APPLY TO MARTIAL ARTS?

Endurance, both aerobic and anaerobic, is an integral part of every martial artist's training. Just taking part in a one hour class requires a minimum level of cardiovascular and musclar endurance. Getting involved in more intense activities like sparring and grappling require even higher levels of endurance capabilities.

Endurance is found in many forms in the martial arts. Muscular endurance is needed for conditioning exercises, forms performance, and kicking and striking drills. Aerobic endurance is necessary for long workouts, heavy bag practice and day long tournaments. Anaerobic endurance is found in dozens of activities like combination attacks, self-defense scenarios and intense ground fighting.

HOW TO IMPROVE

Aerobic conditioning

Aerobic endurance can be improved substantially through training. Aerobic endurance training should consist of at least two to three periods a week during which you reach and sustain seventy percent of your maximum heart rate for twenty to thirty minutes. This level can be estimated as the point at which you are breathing hard but not so strenuously that you cannot carry on a causal conversation during the exercise.

The best exercises for cardiovascular conditioning are those that use large muscle groups and are somewhat rhythmic, like running, bicycling, jumping rope and swimming. As your cardiovascular capacity increases, you must intensify your workout to reach the same seventy percent threshold. This means that your fitness level is improving.

Interval training

Anaerobic endurance is best improved through interval training. Interval training is an exercise program where short, intense bursts of exercise are interspersed with periods of active rest. Active rest can be any light exercise that maintains an aerobic endurance level heart rate. Active rest serves to cleanse the lactic acid build-up that takes place in the muscles during the anaerobic energy production of the intense activity phases. An example of interval training would be to spar one minute nonstop on the heavy bag then spend three minutes doing light footwork exercises. By repeating this sequence several times, you achieve the benefits of interval training.

Interval training works both the aerobic and anaerobic systems. During the intense activity, the anaerobic system is taxed and during the active rest period, the aerobic system is worked. By requiring your body to shift rapidly from one method to the other, you gain greater benefits than with aerobic or anaerobic exercise alone. The stress placed on your cardiovascular system as it escalates and relaxes during interval training is crucial to developing endurance for martial arts.

Interval training places more value on the benefits derived from the interval between activity bursts more than from the intense activity itself. For this reason, a fifty minute workout consisting of eight five minute bursts of exercises with a few minutes rest in between is more effective than fifty minutes of continuous aerobic-type exercise.

Interval training can also be used to develop speed. For speed workouts, use a maximum number of repetitions in a short time with a long active rest period. *Example*: Do as many heavy bag kicks as you can in one minute then rest for five minutes. For endurance benefits, lengthen the period of intensive activity and shorten the rest. *Example*: Sprint one hundred yards, jog back, then sprint again.

Circuit training

Often confused with interval training, circuit training is good for improving muscular endurance. Circuit training consists of periods of aerobic activity interspersed with exercises to improve muscular strength and endurance. *Example*: Fifty push-ups followed by three minutes of jumping rope followed by fifty push-ups and so on with a variety of exercises.

Circuit training is so named because it is often set up as a number of stations where the athlete has to complete a certain exercise at each station. For martial arts training, a circuit might consists of ten stations, each with a designated exercise like sit-ups, push-ups, jumping-jacks, target kicking, heavy bag kicking, etc. Students move around the room at designated intervals and perform the exercises indicated at each station until everyone completes one rotation.

9-1 Distance running   i p

Correct execution: Run for a distance of one to five miles at medium speed.

Variation: 9-1A Alternate running at medium speed and walking as you feel necessary

Main benefit: Increases cardiovascular endurance

Also improves: lower body strength

Martial arts applications: Improves the ability to exercise or practice over a long period of time. Also improves kicking and footwork.

Cautions: If you develop pain in your knees, ankles or shins take some time off. If the condition persists discontinue running and consult a specialist. Running has a high risk of injury and reinjury.

9-2 Swimming   i p e

Correct execution: Swim laps for fifteen to thirty minutes in a pool or other body of water. Good for those with joint injuries that make running painful.

Main benefit: Improves cardiovascular endurance

Also improves: upper body strength

Martial arts applications: Improves the ability to exercise or practice over a long period of time. Also improves power in upper body skills.

Cautions: Never swim without prior instruction. Always swim with a partner or under proper supervision.

9-3 Bicycling   i p e

Correct execution: Bicycle for fifteen to thirty minutes on a stationary or road bike.

Main benefit: Improves cardiovascular endurance

Also improves: lower body strength, speed

Martial arts applications: Improves the ability to exercise or practice over a long period of time. Also improves kicking skills.

Cautions: Use caution and wear proper safety gear when bicycling on roadways.

9-4 Heavy bag workout   i g e

Correct execution: Spar three to five rounds of three minutes each with the heavy bag. Focus on simple skills.

Main benefit: Improves cardiovascular endurance

Also improves: strength, timing, accuracy

Martial arts applications: Improves the accuracy and power of striking and kicking.

Caution: Striking the heavy bag with force has a high risk of injury. Use caution in heavy bag training and avoid circular skills that require a follow-through like axe kick and hook kick.

9-5 Interval training   i g

Correct execution: Spar with the heavy bag for three minutes then spend two minutes of active rest practicing footwork. Repeat as many times as you feel comfortable.

Variations: **9-5A** Sprint one hundred yards and jog back to the start
9-5B Three minutes of focus glove drills followed by one minute of stretching
9-5C Spar three minute rounds with a one minute rest between

Main benefit: Improves anaerobic endurance

Also improves: aerobic endurance, strength, speed

Martial arts applications: Prepares you for activities like sparring and self-defense that require intense bursts of activity interspersed with periods of light activity.

9-6 Tree sparring   i e

Correct execution: Run at medium speed along a wooded area. When you approach a low hanging branch spend about thirty seconds throwing quick, simple attacks at it. Then continue running and repeat.

Main benefit: Improves anaerobic endurance

Also improves: aerobic endurance, speed, timing, accuracy

Martial arts applications: Improves endurance and sparring skills

Cautions: Do not kick tree trunks or small trees because repeated abuse causes them to die. Stick to the thin branches that snap back easily when touched.

9-7 Stair running   i e

Correct execution: Run up one to a dozen flights of stairs at full speed then walk or jog back down.

Variation: 9-7A Run uphill

Main benefit: Improves anaerobic endurance

Also improves: aerobic endurance, speed, strength

Martial arts applications: Improves endurance for intense activities like sparring and self-defense.

Cautions: Never run down stairs because it is too stressful for the knees and ankles. Stair running is very intensive and should be taken slowly at first.

9-8 In place running   i g

Correct execution: Run in place for sixty seconds at a time, raising your knees up as high and as quickly as you can with every step.

Variation: 9-8A Run forward in the same manner

Main benefit: Anaerobic endurance

Also improves: speed, strength, aerobic endurance

Martial arts applications: Improves kicking skills and endurance for intensive activities

9-9 Sparring   i p g e

Correct execution: Spar with a partner for one to five rounds of three minutes each.

Variations: 9-9A In a class, rotate partners for sparring matches of one minute each.
9-9B If you do not have a partner, shadow spar.

Main benefit: Improves anaerobic endurance

Also improves: aerobic endurance, speed, timing

Martial arts applications: Improves sparring skills

Cautions: Always use proper protection gear and respect the rules set by your instructor or your partner and yourself.

TRACKING YOUR PROGRESS

The following are some sample exercises you can use to track your progress. You may make copies of these pages for your records.

1. Select an aerobic endurance exercise and record the amount of time you spend in continuous exercise each training session.

Aerobic Endurance exercise _____

DATE	TIME	DATE	TIME

TRACKING YOUR PROGRESS

2. Select an interval training exercise and record the type of exercise and the number of sets you do each day.

Interval exercise _____

DATE	SETS	DATE	SETS

INSTRUCTOR'S NOTES

① Because endurance training takes a significant amount of time each day, encourage your students to do their endurance work outside of class. You can provide an appropriate space and help them design a program so that the actual class time can focus on skill training rather than on endurance work.

② Avoid introducing new skills when students are tired. New skills require fresh muscles to practice them correctly and fresh minds to monitor feedback and make the necessary adjustments for learning to take place.

10

ACCURACY

WHAT IS IT?

Accuracy is the ability to carry out movements with precision. An accurate movement is one that fulfills its goal without deviation. There are varying degrees of accuracy, ranging from perfect, as in hitting the bull's eye, to acceptable, like just hitting the target. The goal of every movement is to create an accurate execution.

WHERE DOES IT COME FROM?

Accuracy comes from the precise execution of movements by corresponding muscles. Muscle spindles, which act in concert with skeletomotor neurons, play a large role in checking and controlling precision movements. By working in unison, they can provide error correction in muscular contraction in less than half the amount of time required for visual reactions.

Muscle spindles are bundles of sensory receptors and muscle fiber that run parallel to and move with muscles to detect muscle length and speed of extension. They are found in larger numbers in muscles used for precision movements than in those used in gross motor activity. For example, the hand muscles contain more than ten times as many muscle spindles per gram of muscle than the large muscles that make up the calf. This abundance of sensory receptors allows the hand to perform delicate precision movements that cannot be duplicated by the larger muscles of the leg.

Spindles make up a significant part of the body's system for checking the accuracy of the muscle's execution of commands sent from the central nervous system. The spindles provide a rich sensory environment that sends detailed feedback to the central nervous system, which then processes it and makes adjustments in the strength and length of contractions made by the muscles.

Precision movements are also controlled by the type of muscle engaged in the activity. Small muscle groups, like those in the hand, have a very low activation threshold. By exerting only small amount of force, they can perform simple tasks. When a task requires greater force, larger muscle groups are recruited and the level of precision is reduced. The largest muscle groups, those that produce maximum tension, are also the least refined, making them more difficult to control. This is why large, powerful movements are most suitable for gross motor skills.

When executing precision movements, small muscle groups and low tension levels are most useful. When executing power movements, expect some loss in accuracy.

HOW DOES IT APPLY TO MARTIAL ARTS?

Accuracy in striking arts, means hitting your opponent or your target correctly. In throwing and grappling arts, it means applying a sure grip to the correct part of the opponent and following through with precision. Accuracy is essential in the sense that if you miss, your energy is wasted, and wasting energy is not smart in any physical activity.

Accuracy is not only the result of the movement, but the execution as well. A technique that is performed accurately uses less energy, moves faster and has more power than poorly performed techniques. Accurate execution results in an accurate outcome.

HOW TO IMPROVE

Accuracy should be developed early in the learning process. When learning anything new, concentrate on imitating a perfect model of the movement as closely as possible. By executing correctly from the beginning, you avoid bad habits that detract from your performance. Accuracy promotes speed and power while minimizing the risk of injury caused by improper technique.

Always practice movements exactly as they will be performed in your target activity. If you practice half heartedly, your actual performance will be the same. Don't expect to go through the motions in practice then dazzle your opponent in the ring. Practice trains the neuromuscular response and the coordination of the brain and the muscles. If you train them poorly, they become conditioned to perform poorly.

Never practice precision skills when you are physically or mentally tired. Tired muscles perform below par, creating a below par muscle memory with each movement you practice. Accuracy is reduced greatly by muscle fatigue. It is reduced even further by mental fatigue. Low concentration can destroy your best efforts at practice. If you are tired, take a break or come back tomorrow. Better to delay perfection one day than to create bad habits that take weeks to undo.

10-1 Fast Point Sparring   p g e

Correct execution: The first person to score in a sparring match is the winner. To encourage accuracy, count only perfect, unblocked attacks as points.

Variation: **10-1A** In a group class , students face each other in pairs, deciding among themselves who is the winner. As a winner is decided, each pair sits. When all pairs are seated, rotate so everyone is facing a new partner and begin again.

Main benefit: Improves accuracy

Also improves: speed, coordination, perception

Martial arts applications: Improves accuracy in attacking

Cautions: Always use proper protection gear when sparring. This drill is intended for intermediate and advanced students only.

10-2 Dynamic Tension   i g

Correct execution: Perform a movement or series of movements slowly but with full tension in every stage of the movement.

Main benefit: Improves accuracy

Also improves: strength

Martial arts applications: Stresses muscles while executing a perfect replica of the target movement, creating a model for the brain to follow during full power executions.

Dynamic tension

10-3 Bar practice   i g e

Correct execution: Holding a wall mounted bar for support, slowly and smoothly execute kicks.

Variation: 10-3 Add tension to the movement.

Main benefit: Improves kicking accuracy

Also improves: strength, balance

Martial arts applications: Creates muscle memory and strength through slow but correct execution of kicks.

10-4 Prone kicking   i g

Correct execution: 1. Lie on your side with your legs outstretched. 2. Raise your top knee and chamber it for side kick. 3. Slowly extend your leg into side kick position and hold.

Variations: **10-4A** Roundhouse kick
                    10-4B Hook kick

Main benefit: Improves kicking accuracy

Also improves: strength, coordination

Martial arts applications: Improves kicking by strengthening leg muscles and creating muscle memory in the kicking leg.

10-5 Focus Pad Training   p g e

Correct execution: One partner holds the focus gloves in position for a specific strike and the other partner strikes the pad with accurate, powerful strikes.

Variation: **10-5** The pads can be varied for different strikes and different heights.

Main benefit: Improves attacking accuracy

Also improves: strength, speed, timing, endurance

Martial arts applications: Improves accuracy in striking and kicking.

10-6 Hanging target drill   i e

Correct execution: Suspend a small target such as a tennis ball, balloon or paper by a string. Practice randomly attacking the target as it swings freely. Concentrate on speed and accuracy.

Main benefit: Improves attacking accuracy

Also improves: speed, coordination, timing

Martial arts applications: Creates light, accurate movements for speedy attacks.

TRACKING YOUR PROGRESS

1. Point sparring (# 10-1)

DATE	OPPONENT	WINS	LOSSES

TRACKING YOUR PROGRESS

2. Focus pads (# 10-5)

DATE	STRIKE/KICK	REPETITIONS

INSTRUCTOR'S NOTES

① Accuracy drills can be boring. Rotate slow drills with fast paced drills. Divide the class into two groups. Have one group practice on the bar while the other does target kicking with the same kick. Rotate stations several times to break up the monotony. When students do poorly in target kicking, suggest points to practice while at the bar to keep everyone focused.

② Be careful in fast point sparring. Overanxious students rush in wildly, leading to a high potential for injury. Start with advanced students who understand the dangers of rushing to attack. Let them demonstrate quick points and emphasize that scoring requires strategy as well as speed.

③ Dynamic tension drills, especially forms practice, are good for cooldown exercises at the end of class. They are slow moving, yet require concentration and exertion. Use them as a type of moving meditation.

11

TIMING

WHAT IS IT?

Timing is the ability to recognize an opportunity and capitalize on it at the perfect moment. Timing is often confused with speed. To clarify, speed is the amount of time it takes for a strike to move from initiation to the target. Timing is moving at the correct moment and tempo. It often requires speed, but is not identical to moving quickly. Timing can be slow, medium or fast.

WHERE DOES IT COME FROM?

Timing comes from a combination of experience and knowledge. Beginners often assume the key to attacking successfully is to strike as quickly as possible at any time. As they advance, they find that speed is not everything. Certain times are better for attacking than others. When a student masters timing, he instinctively senses the perfect time for an attack. The mechanics of timing can be learned through the use of simple principles. The actual execution of perfect timing, however, can only be learned through long, hard practice.

Timing in action is a blend of speed, perception and accuracy. It also requires superb technical knowledge and control. Confidence in your ability and self-knowledge enhance your physical skills and lure your opponent into your preferred timing. Knowing when, how and with what weapon to strike is the essence of timing.

HOW DOES IT APPLY TO MARTIAL ARTS?

Timing lies at the heart of martial skills. In every fight from a full scale war to a street fight, the side with superior timing has a significant advantage. Timing separates the good fighters from the great fighters. Timing scores knockouts, wins battles and defeats superior opponents.

One of the reasons timing is so important lies in controlling the distance between you and your opponent. By moving at the right speed and the right time, you can avoid incoming attacks and launch initiative and counterattacks successfully.

In every attack, there is a time at which the attacker makes himself vulnerable to a counterattack. Movement creates weaknesses in form and defense. Through these weaknesses even a superior opponent can be defeated. Knowing what the weakness is and taking advantage of it is the key to victory.

HOW TO IMPROVE

Timing can be improved through practice, drills and experience. Perfecting drills without experience is like having a shiny new car and never taking it out of the driveway. You may enjoy the admiring looks from the neighbors, but you'll never know the joys of cruising on the open road. Conversely, experience without systemized practice requires so much learning from trial and error, you may never get beyond the basics.

Practice means repetition of the basics of your system so you can use them at will. Once you have a grasp of the basics, move on to arranged drills.

Drills can be done alone, with equipment or with a partner. The best drills are those that simulate actual sparring, grappling or whatever situation you expect to encounter. By simulating your target activity, you practice the actual timing skills you need without extraneous activity.

BASIC PRINCIPLES IN TIMING:

1. Attack when your opponent is:
   a. in midstep
   b. changing stance
   c. advancing
   d. retreating
   e. reacting to a feint
   f. stationary
   g. thinking or distracted

2. Counterattack when your opponent is:
   a. changing position or direction
   b. spinning or turning
   c. attacking
   d. between attacks
   e. finishing an attack
   f. retreating after an attack

Based on these principles, design drills that hone your timing skills.

Attention to detail rounds out training for improved timing. Avoid telegraphing your initiation movements. Remove any pre-initiation habits, like shouting or foot stamping, that signal your initiative attack. Use swift and varied footwork to control the timing of your opponent's movements.

Take every opportunity to create or seize the perfect time for an attack or counterattack.

11-1 Visualization   i g

Correct execution: With your eyes closed, imagine how you would react to a specific attack or situation. See your reaction in a detailed, slow motion sequence. After visualization, practice what you imagined, trying to closely imitate your vision.

Main benefit: Improves timing

Also improves: accuracy

Martial arts applications: Sharpens reaction skills and improves sparring.

11-2 Broken rhythm drill   i p

Correct execution: Practice any technique at a slower than normal or off tempo speed. Instead of going full speed throughout the technique, try starting out slowly then speeding up in mid-attack or starting quickly and slowing as your opponent reacts. The results will be quite surprising.

Main benefit: Creates variety in timing

Martial arts applications: Broken rhythm confuses the opponent and allows you to vary your attacks.

11-3 Reaction drill   p g

Correct execution: Facing a partner, practice simple attack and counter combinations. *Example*: Partner A does a right roundhouse kick and partner B counters with right roundhouse kick. Work on the correct timing of each attack and counter. Countering too soon results in jamming and countering too late results in missing. Experiment with as many combinations as you can develop.

Main benefit: Improves reaction timing

Also improves: speed, perception, agility

Martial arts applications: Improves sparring skills

11-4 Heavy bag workout   i e

Correct execution: Let the bag swing freely and attack it at random. Concentrate on the timing of the bag's movement. Move around and mix in footwork with attacking and defending skills. Do not stop the bag and try not to wait too long between attacks. Practice going with the movement of the bag.

Main benefit: Improves timing

Also improves: agility, speed, power, accuracy

Martial arts applications: Improves sparring skills

Cautions: Heavy bag training has a high risk of injury. Use caution in striking and kicking the bag with force.

11-5 Speed Bag workout   i e

Correct execution: Strike a speed bag with rhythmic strikes. Concentrate on keeping the same rhythm without form breaks.

Variation: 11-5A Can be done with continuous kicking, by not dropping the leg between kicks.

Main benefit: Improves rhythmic timing

Also improves: accuracy, speed, perception

Martial arts applications: Improves sparring skills and lightness of strikes and kicks.

Kicking the speed bag (11-5A)

11-6 Double end bag workout   i e

Correct execution: Strike a double ended bag or ball concentrating on continuous action and rhythmic movements. Move with the bag and strike it from whatever angle and with whatever skill required to keep up a smooth flow of attacks.

Main benefit: Improves reaction timing

Also improves: Accuracy, perception, speed

Martial arts applications: Improves continuity in attacks and builds quick responses to varying situations.

Striking the double end bag

11-7 Sparring   p g e

Correct execution: Spar with a variety of partners to develop timing that applies to a wide assortment of situations and personal styles. Every individual uses different attacks and different timing.

Main benefit: Improves timing

Also improves: endurance, perception, speed, accuracy

Martial arts applications: Improves sparring skills

Cautions: Always use adequate protection gear when sparring.

Sparring with protection gear

11-8 Individual practice   i e

Correct execution: Spend time alone to practice. Most practice is done in group or class environments, yet timing requires you to become more in touch with yourself and your personal style and habits. By training alone, you develop a deeper sense of your strengths and weaknesses as well as your inner timing.

Variation: 11-8A Practice on various types of equipment and pay special attention to your thinking and the precision of your movements.

Main benefit: Improves inner timing

Also improves: perception, mental strength

Martial arts applications: Improves almost every aspect of your training by creating a stronger link between your brain and body.

Caution: When practicing alone, stick to safe skills. Skills with a high risk of injury should always be practiced under proper supervision.

TRACKING YOUR PROGRESS

You'll know when you've got it!

You'll know when you've got it!

You'll know when you've got it!

INSTRUCTOR'S NOTES

① Timing skills should be introduced in the intermediate stage and drilled in the advanced and black belt stages. Timing usually develops after basic skills have matured into the automatic phase.

② Timing practice is essential for developing skill in sparring or activities that require diverse, unplanned responses.

③ Timing practice should be done with partners whenever possible to develop a realistic sense of the relatively fluctuating combat situation.

12

MENTAL STRENGTH & ENDURANCE

WHAT IS IT?

A proper state of mind is essential to achieve peak effectiveness in physical performance. Every physical action originates from the central nervous system, which is directed and overseen by the brain. When the mind is properly trained, the potential for optimum performance is greater. Mental training can be divided into two categories, mental strength and mental endurance.

Mental strength encompasses characteristics like intensity, courage, fortitude, will, spirit, conscientiousness, competency and mastery. A strong mind gives you the ability to concentrate on given tasks, initiate training responsibilities, undertake challenges, overcome obstacles, determine principles, take on a superior opponent and set high goals.

Mental endurance is characterized by attributes like stamina, discipline, determination, patience, perseverance, resoluteness and tenacity. Psychological endurance gives you the energy to stick to a demanding training schedule, overcome slumps, complete monotonous drills, win out over a stubborn opponent, finish what you start and reach your goals.

Mental endurance and strength are what separates the best from the rest. In any sport or physical discipline, thousands of athletes have world class skills, but only a few have world class minds.

HOW DOES IT APPLY TO MARTIAL ARTS?

One of the premier reasons for mental strength and endurance in martial arts training is to overcome the opponent. Whether your opponent is a bully, a mugger, a competitor or a training partner, a strong mind is a prerequisite for confronting and overcoming a challenge to your physical safety. Without a strong mindset, your first instinct is to escape or submit in the face of danger.

Mental strength is also need to undertake the strenuous and often seemingly impossible demands of training. Martial arts classes are notorious for challenging even the most physically fit students. Determination to better yourself or learn something new is essential in beginning each new stage of training.

Mental endurance is necessary to stick to your training schedule, especially when it becomes boring or difficult. Improvement comes only through practice and repetition, which is often a lonely endeavor. With no team to fall back on and nobody to blame for your mistakes, martial arts can be especially hard to stick to when the going gets rough.

HOW TO IMPROVE

One of the most common beliefs about martial arts is that they develop a strong mind as well as a strong body. Depending on the student and instructor, this can be as true or as false as in any other sport. How much psychological development results from your martial arts training is largely up to you. What you get out of mental training exercises is directly related to what you put into them.

As in physical conditioning, mental training must be purposeful and goal oriented. Self-discipline are not an automatic benefit of martial arts training. Behaving during training exactly as you do in other daily events will not bring changes. Approaching every action and exercise in the training hall with determination and seriousness will result in new habits that carry over into your daily life.

WHERE DOES IT COME FROM?

Mental fortitude is a predominantly innate characteristic. Some people are naturally stubborn, disciplined, determined or strong willed. If these inherent qualities are directed appropriately, they result in mental strength and endurance. If they are misdirected, they result in mental rigidity and single mindedness. If you are naturally determined and disciplined, work on harnessing and directing your instinctive behavior toward positive results.

If you are doubtful, hesitant, reluctant, timid or generally not disciplined and determined, there are ways to strengthen your mind if you choose to. The key is that you have to want to improve. Once you make up your mind to become more confident, martial arts training and the exercises in this chapter will be very helpful. In fact, mental strength and endurance are the characteristics that have the most potential for improvement. The human spirit, unlike the human body, is boundless.

12-1 Visualization   i g

Correct execution: After learning a new movement, sit quietly with your eyes closed and see yourself performing the movement perfectly. When you visualize each movement, concentrate on every detail to enhance the realism.

Variation: 12-1A Watch a new or difficult movement performed by an expert on video. Immediately close your eyes and see your-self doing the same movement, as if it is you on the video.

Main benefit: Improves competency and mastery skills

Also improves: accuracy, perception

Martial arts applications: Visualizing movements creates activity in the brain similar to the activity that takes place when you actually perform the movement. By stimulating your thought patterns, you enhance your perception of the movement.

12-2 Relaxation   i g

Correct execution: Sit or lie in comfortable position. Beginning with your feet, consciously tense and relax your foot muscles. Next move to your legs and so on through your body. When you can actively tense and relax each area, try to relax without first tensing.

Variation: 12-2A Just before executing a simple movement, consciously relax the body parts involved.

Main benefit: Improves discipline and patience

Also improves: speed

Martial arts applications: Through conscious relaxation, you improve the communication between the nervous system and muscles. Relaxation before execution also fosters speed of initiation and execution by clearing the pathways between the nerves and muscles.

12-3 Meditation   i g

Correct execution: Sit in a relaxed, upright posture. Close your eyes and breath naturally but deeply. Let your mind go freely, not trying to think of anything in particular and not trying to remove your thought. Start with a short period like five minutes and increase the length of time as you become more comfortable.

Variation: **12-3A** Meditation can also be active, such as during form performance or repetitive drills. Try to be totally in sync with the movements, without extraneous thoughts.

Main benefit: Improves mental endurance

Also improves: perception

Martial arts applications: Meditation is an excellent counterpart to the vigorous and often fierce techniques of martial arts.

12-4 Breathing exercises   i g

Correct execution: Sit in an upright posture with your spine straight and chest open. Breathe in slowly to the count of eight, hold briefly and breathe out again to the count of eight. Concentrate on breathing deeply and evenly.

Variation: 12-4A Use the breathing exercise during slow and focused exercises.

Main benefit: Improves mental endurance

Also improves: endurance

Martial arts applications: Deep breathing exercises focus your mind and put you in touch with your body rhythms. Breathing exercises during movements intensify the dynamic quality of every movement while relaxing your mind and body.

12-5 Repetition drill   i

Correct execution: Select a skill you want to improve. Spend a one hour training session to practice only that skill. Practice slowly, quickly, with equipment, with footwork, in combination with other skills. Repeat the skill as many times and in as many ways as you can imagine.

Main benefit: Mental endurance

Also improves: endurance

Martial arts applications: By focusing intensely on a single skill, you not only improve, but you may discover many new applications and attributes of that technique. The key is to practice intently without distraction.

12-6 Psyching up   i

Correct execution: To prepare for an event, practice psyching up. The most common way of psyching for an event is through a combination of exercise and visualization. After your warm-up, do some light, rhythmic exercise like bouncing/jogging in place, jumping rope or footwork. As you exercise, visualize your successful performance over and over.

Variations: **12-6A** Use a favorite piece of music
                     12-6B Repeat a motivational saying
                     12-6C Use positive self-talk

Main benefit: Improves mental strength

Martial arts applications: By practicing psyching up before your regular workout, you can develop a pattern that your body recognizes and responds to.

INSTRUCTOR'S NOTES

① Mental training at the beginner and intermediate stages should consist primarily of encouraging self-discipline in classroom activities and promoting concentration exercises like meditation and breathing. When students reach the advanced stage or show an interest in more intense training, begin to intensify the mental training requirements. An overabundance of mental training exercises however can intimidate beginners and turn away potentially good students.

② Mental condition is apt to be affected in a negative way by emotion and stress. By creating a calm and stress-free training environment, you can enhance the effects of training. A calm and stress-free environment means a place where your students can enjoy training without unnecessary distractions from yourself or others.

13

NUTRITION

Contrary to popular belief, there is no magic supplement or diet that creates outstanding athletes. Athletes' needs are very similar to those of nonathletes when it comes to nutrition. Athletes, like nonathletes, need daily supplies of carbohydrates, fats, proteins, vitamins, minerals and water. The major difference is that athletes, depending on their level of activity, require more of everything. Their bodies work harder during exercise, causing them to burn more calories and use up energy supplies faster.

THE COMPONENTS OF GOOD NUTRITION

Protein

What does it do?

Protein builds tissues, especially muscle tissue. Tissue growth is an ongoing process and requires a steady supply of protein. Storing up large amounts of protein in an effort to improve muscle development quickly is ineffective because protein in excess of fifteen to twenty percent of the diet is excreted as waste and protein has little immediate effect on muscle tissue. Eat a diet that provides a regular supply of protein for best results.

How much do you need?

Protein should make up ten to fifteen percent of your daily calories. Choose high protein foods carefully, because high protein often equals high fat.

Where does it come from?

There are two types of protein: animal protein and vegetable protein. Animal protein is found in foods like eggs, lean meat, milk and cheese. Vegetable protein is found in foods like wheat, rye, and green vegetables.

Fats

What do they do?

Fats provide energy to muscles during prolonged periods of exercise. Initially, the body relies on carbohydrates. As exercise intensifies or continues, especially beyond one hour, fats become increasingly important sources of energy. You should not, however, eat fatty foods just before exercising.

Fats require three to five hours of digestion, which reduces the physical output capacity of the body and creates a general feeling of lethargy.

How much do you need?

Fats, preferably unsaturated, should make up twenty-five percent or less of total daily calories.

Where does it come from?

Foods that are high in fat include fish, butter, cream, bacon, sausage and fried foods.

Carbohydrates

What do they do?

The primary function of carbohydrates is to provide a continuous supply of energy to cells. They are readily available, as in the form of glucose, and are the first form of energy expended during activity.

How much do you need?

Carbohydrates should make up fifty to sixty percent of daily calories.

Where do they come from?

There are two types of carbohydrates: simple and complex. Simple carbohydrates have only one or two sugar molecules and are found in fresh fruit, soda, candy and cookies. With the exception of fresh fruit, it is best to avoid these sugary foods before exercise because high sugar foods lead to feelings of fatigue and heaviness. Complex carbohydrates have many sugar molecules and are found in vegetables, brown rice, whole grain breads, cereals, beans and dry nuts.

Vitamins and Minerals

What do they do?

Vitamins are used by cells in small amounts to perform metabolic functions. Minerals are chemicals necessary to promote activities like nerve tissue function and muscle contraction. There is little evidence to support claims that large doses of vitamins or minerals increase performance significantly.

How much do you need?

Vitamin and mineral requirements vary from person to person. You can obtain recommended levels for specific elements from your doctor.

Where do they come from?

A properly balanced diet provides all of the vitamins and minerals necessary for the average person. Supplements are not necessary unless a deficiency is evident. Supplements should only be taken under the supervised care of a medical professional because large doses of certain elements can be toxic or even fatal.

Water

What does it do?

Water is used to transport nutrients and waste products in the body. It is also necessary for metabolism and temperature regulation. An inadequate supply of water, called dehydration, slows body function and severely impairs performance.

How much do you need?

The human body is fifty-five to sixty percent water and some of that water is lost through sweat during exercise. Drink plenty of fluids during and after exercise, at least eight glasses a day. Do not wait until you feel thirsty to begin replenishing fluids.

Where does it come from?

Water, in its natural state, is the best replacement for lost fluids. Sports drinks, while good post-activity refreshers, are not recommended during exercise. Sports drinks are high in glucose, a carbohydrate, and even small amounts of carbohydrates slow the transfer of fluids from the stomach to the intestine. Slow transfer means slow absorption into the body and less water available for the bodily functions critical to peak performance like waste removal and temperature control.

NUTRITIONAL CONCERNS OF ATHLETES

Adequate diet

An adequate diet comes from eating a variety of foods from the four food groups. The average daily caloric requirement for adults is twenty-seven hundred calories for men and twenty-one hundred calories for women. Athletes will require more calories depending on the intensity and frequency with which they exercise. When planning your training diet be sure to include the following every day:

Milk/milk products	2-3 servings
Meat/High protein	2-3 servings
Vegetables/Fruit	7-10 servings
Cereal/Grains	6-10 servings

Pre-exercise meal

Before an important event or strenuous practice, eat a light low-fat, low-sugar, low-protein, high carbohydrate meal and allow two to three hours for digestion.

Diet and endurance

The type of fuel necessary for muscular contraction depends on the intensity and duration of the activity in which you participate. During continuous, moderate activity, the energy for muscular contraction is provided mainly by the body's fat and carbohydrate stores. If activity continues and glycogen stores in the liver are depleted, a greater percentage of energy is derived from the breakdown of fat.

Although low levels of glycogen lead to fatigue, the fatigue occurs only in the muscles that are active. Inactive muscles retain their glycogen supply. Drinking a solution of glucose in water, the common base of sports drinks, can prolong exercise for a short time, but energy production becomes severely limited.

Repeated periods of strenuous training can bring on fatigue due to the gradual depletion of the body's carbohydrate stories, making exercise more and more difficult. After prolonged or strenuous exercise, allow at least forty-eight hours and ensure sufficient carbohydrate intake to restore glycogen in the muscles to preexercise levels.

Normal glycogen levels can be maintained by eating carbohydrates equal to fifty to sixty percent of daily calories. "Carbohydrate loading," eating carbohydrates in larger amounts, is highly effective for athletes in endurance sports like marathoning. For the average athlete, including martial artists, it adds little to overall performance.

14

INJURY
PREVENTION

An injury to any part of your body can pose a serious threat to your training program. While many injuries are treatable, treatment is often like taping a piece of torn paper back together. It may be one piece again, but it's just not the same as before. The best medicine is to avoid injuries through smart training practices.

This chapter lists important tips for staying injury free through many years of training. Although you will be injured from time to time no matter how careful you are, you can avoid many injuries through caution and planning.

SAFETY IN THE TRAINING AREA

1. Always practice in areas suitable for your activity. The best practice areas have:

> **Plenty of space**
> **Good light**
> **Adequate ventilation**
> **Flat, sturdy floors** - padded for impact skills
> **Enough room** per person
> **Good temperature** - between fifty-five and seventy-two degrees Fahrenheit. Lower temperatures for intense activity and higher for moderate activity.

2. Use padded surfaces or mats for falling, throwing and ground practice.

3. Keep a first aid kit in the workout area and be familiar with first aid procedures.

4. Keep training equipment in good repair and thoroughly examine it before each use, especially if the equipment is used by many other people.

5. Avoid exercise in extreme heat and humidity or extreme cold.

BEFORE YOU BEGIN

1. Always warm-up for at least ten to fifteen minutes.

2. Avoid exercise when ill or fatigued. This is a leading cause of injury.

3. Strengthen and stretch muscles thoroughly to prevent stress injuries in the joints, especially the knees and ankles.

4. Have a thorough physical exam before beginning a new exercise program.

DURING YOUR WORKOUT

1. Follow safety precautions for each activity and exercise.

2. Begin new exercises cautiously until you understand and become accustomed them.

3. Practice within your range of ability. Do not try to imitate people who are much better than you, without proper instruction.

4. Use properly fitting protection gear for activities that entail or may result in contact. Common protection gear includes:

> Protection cup (men)
> Shin guards
> Arm guards
> Head gear with or without face mask
> Chest protector
> Gloves/hand guards
> Padded boots/instep guards

5. Train left and right sides equally to prevent domination of one side over the other.

6. Train opposing muscles (i.e. stomach and back) equally to prevent domination of one group.

7. Move and land on flexed knees to absorb impact.

8. Stay relaxed.

9. Never hold your breath during exercise. Inhale during extension movements and exhale during recovery and flexion movements.

10. Always spend ten to fifteen minutes for cool-down exercises.

WORKING WITH A PARTNER

1. Train with partners who are similar or slightly better than you in physical condition or skill level. Your partner should push you but not so much that you cannot keep up most of the time.

2. Take advice or instruction only from qualified people.

3. Always use a spotter when working with equipment or doing high risk exercises (like hand stands).

STAYING FIT

1. Avoid rapid weight loss or gain.

2. Do not overtrain. Overtraining causes staleness and even regression. If you feel like you need a day off, listen to your body.

3. Provide immediate care for injures.

4. If injured, rest until you have no pain or swelling and have regained your normal range of motion and strength.

OVERUSE INJURIES

Overuse injuries are those caused by continuous abuse of a muscle, joint or physical structure without appropriate rest or recovery time. Overuse injuries are common in athletes who perform a limited number of repetitive actions in every workout. Runners, tennis players and baseball pitchers are good examples of athletes with high rates of overuse injuries. In runners, the knees go first, with pitchers it's the shoulder and with tennis players, the elbows degenerate quickly. Overuse injuries creep up on you slowly and rarely go away unless you stop the injury-producing movements.

Common causes of the **circumstances that lead to overuse injuries** are:

1. Involved in one sport too intensively
2. Pushing too hard for your ability level
3. Use of same routine every day
4. Exercising even though tired, ill, injured, etc.

Overuse injuries can be lessened or prevented when they are caught early. Some **signs of an impending overuse injury** are:

1. Pain or stiffness during exercise
2. Pain or stiffness during normal activities
3. General fatigue or malaise
4. Poor overall performance, feeling of being in a slump
5. Frequent illness
6. Obsession with one sport
7. Desire to win at any cost
8. Lack of identity outside the sport
9. Poor concentration, feeling restless and distracted

If you can identify more than three of the above warning signs in yourself, it is time to reevaluate your training. Some ways of getting back on track are:

1. Take some time off or alternate days of training.
2. Quit competition for a while and train for self-fulfillment.
3. Talk to your instructor or coach for objective advice.

15

SAMPLE WORKOUTS

This chapter contains sample workouts for developing power, flexibility, speed, endurance, physical integration and mental strength.   These plans provide a general guide from which you can shape your personalized training plan.   Each workout is designed to present a balanced sample of results oriented exercises.

The workouts are categorized by experience level. The beginner workout is intended for those with no experience up to those with one year of experience. The intermediate plan is geared to those with one to four years of experience, or up to black belt level. The advanced plan is geared toward those students who have at least five years experience.

To find the best level for you, start with the beginner plan and slowly work your way up to a challenging workout.

Designing your personalized workout

1. Start with the beginner workout in each section and select the type and number of exercises that are best for you. Each successive plan gives you an idea of how much to increase each exercise and which exercises to add or drop as you progress. Again, these are a general guide from which to adapt your personalized plan.

2. There are two ways to organize your daily workouts. You can select a theme for the day, like endurance workouts on Monday, Wednesday and Friday and speed workouts on Tuesday, Thursday and Saturday. Or you can mix some of each type of exercise in every workout. Choose the way that works best for you. If you are not sure which way is better or if you are just beginning, start with a mixed plan.

3. When selecting exercises, it is not necessary to include every exercise suggested. First, eliminate any exercises that may cause or aggravate injuries. If you have weak knees avoid exercises like squats, lunges and jumping. If you have dislocated a shoulder in the past, remove shoulder extension and rotation exercises. See the cautions with each exercise for more specific information.

4. Next, select exercises from the beginner plan that you think will be most beneficial to you based on the type of art you practice. Example: If you use a lot of kicks, concentrate on leg and trunk exercises. If you do a lot of throwing, select arm, chest and back exercises. If you like grappling, choose arm, chest, shoulder and leg exercises. If you are not sure which exercises to choose, list the primary areas of improvement you want and then check the main benefits section of each exercise to see which ones provide the benefits you want to achieve.

5. As you progress, your needs may change. Update your plan monthly. Drop exercises that are no longer producing results and add more challenging exercises. If you need a specific exercise, but are bored with it, look for a variation that provides similar benefits. Or try rotating exercises on a monthly basis. *Example*: One month do knuckle push-ups and the next do regular push-ups. Variations provide variety in both routine and results.

Using the Sample Plans

All of the sample workouts are designed according to a consistent pattern. Each looks like the following:

①	②	③	④	⑤	⑥
Exercises	Reps	Beginner	Intermediate	Advanced	#
Push-ups	10	1	2	3	2-6

Column ① lists the exercise name exactly as it is found in this book. Column ② lists the number of repetitions in one set. Every level does the same number of repetitions in a set. You can do each set with a brief rest in between or you can do all of the sets without stopping. Sets that are timed should be done with a short recovery period between them.

Column ③ lists the number of sets a beginner should do. Columns ④ and ⑤ list the number of sets for intermediate and advanced practitioners respectively. Column ⑥ lists the number of the exercise. The first number is the chapter number, followed by the individual exercise number.

In the example above, the exercise is push-ups. Each set consists of ten repetitions, so   beginners do ten, intermediate students do twenty and advanced students do thirty. Push-ups are the sixth (6) exercise in the second (2) chapter so they are listed with the number 2-6.

INSTRUCTOR'S NOTES

① The sample plans are an excellent guide for designing warm-up and conditioning exercises for your classes. Use the beginner, intermediate and advanced levels as guidelines for appropriate types and amounts of exercises for each level.

② Use a assortment of exercises in each class and rotate types of exercises for variety. Students quickly tire of the same warm-up and conditioning routine night after night. There are enough exercises in this book to design a different plan for every day of the month.

③ On the other hand, do not use too much variety. You should have a core group of exercises like push-ups, sit-ups, stretching, etc. that are consistent throughout every class. Consistency encourages improvement while variety discourages boredom. A perfect balance of both will keep your students on the road to peak fitness and maintain their interest long enough to achieve it.

PHYSICAL INTEGRATION

Physical integration exercises improve coordination, agility and balance.

Exercise	Reps	Beg.	Int.	Adv.	#
25 yard zig-zag run	1	2	4	6	7-2
25 yard shuttle run	1	2	4	6	7-3
25 yard backward run	1	2	4	6	7-4
25 yard knee touch	1	2	4	6	5-3
25 yard side scoop	1	2	4	6	5-4
footwork drill	30 sec.	2	4	6	7-5
jumping jacks	10	3	5	10	5-1
jumping rope	1 min.	2	4	6	5-2
jump (feet to hands)	5	0	2	4	7-1B
jump and split	5	0	2	4	7-1C
star jumps	5	1	2	3	5-6
single leg balance	30 sec.	1	2	3	6-7
single leg stretch	1	2	2	2	6-8
single leg squat	5	1	2	3	6-9
single leg hop	20	1	2	3	6-10

Exercise	Reps	Beg.	Int.	Adv.	#
windmills	5	1	1	2	6-11
horse stance drill	3	2	2	2	6-16
pushing kicks	3	0	2	3	6-5
pulling kicks	3	0	2	3	6-5B
gombae paree	3	1	1	2	6-14
partner bridge	10 sec.	1	2	2	5-15
forward roll	5	1	2	3	5-7
backward roll	5	0	2	3	5-8
spinal roll	5	0	1	2	7-9
partner back roll	5	0	1	2	5-9
back to back stand	5	1	2	2	6-12
bicycles	10	2	4	6	5-11
shoulder stand	10 sec.	1	2	2	7-8
bridge	5	1	2	3	7-10
head stand	10 sec.	1	2	3	6-1
hand stand	10 sec.	0	1	2	6-2
hand stand walking	10 sec.	0	0	1	6-3

ENDURANCE

This sample workout contains only a small number of exercise because endurance exercises are lengthy in nature. Depending on your level, this workout will take between forty-five minutes and two hours to complete. Allow a brief recovery, ideally less than one minute, between sets of three minutes or less in length. For the running, swimming and biking exercises, allow a rest of less than five minutes between sets.

Exercise	Duration	Beg.	Int.	Adv.	#
run, swim, or bike	20 min.	1	2	3	9-1, -2, -3
heavy bag	1 min.	2	5	10	9-4
sparring	3 min.	1	3	5	9-6
in place run	3 min.	1	2	3	9-8
stair run	1 flight	5	10	15	9-7
interval training					9-5B
focus glove	3 min.	1	2	3	
light footwork	1 min.	1	2	3	

POWER

Repetitions are given for one side only. If the number of repetitions for a single arm or single leg exercise is ten, do ten on the right side and ten on the left side. For total body exercises, like push-ups, the number of repetitions given is the total number that should be done.

Exercise	Reps	Beg.	Int.	Adv.	#
fist clench	5	2	3	5	2-3
stick twist	10	1	2	3	2-4
chin-ups	5	1	2	3	2-6
knee-ups	10	1	2	3	2-14
lunges	10	1	2	3	2-16
squats	10	1	2	3	2-17
calf raises	10	1	2	3	2-18
curl-ups	10	1	2	3	2-7
side sit-ups	5	1	2	3	2-9
V-ups	5	2	3	5	2-8
trunk lifts	5	1	2	3	2-11
front bridge	10 sec.	1	2	3	2-1
rear bridge	10 sec.	1	2	3	2-1A
alternate knee raise	5	2	3	4	2-12C

Exercise	Reps	Beg.	Int.	Adv.	#
alternate leg raise	5	2	3	4	2-13A
double leg raise	5	1	3	4	2-13
trunk twist	5	1	2	3	2-13F
scissors	10	1	2	3	2-13D
flutter kicks	10	1	2	3	2-13E
rebound w/partner	5	0	1	2	2-13G
bench leg raises	5	0	1	2	2-13H
push-ups	10	1	2	3	2-2
knuckle push-ups	10	0	1	2	2-2D
rolling push-ups	5	1	2	3	2-2F
partner push-ups	10	0	1	2	2-2G
30 sec. push-ups	5	0	1	2	2-2I
back extension					
arms on back	10	1	2	3	2-10C
arms over head	5	0	1	2	2-10B
raise legs	5	0	1	2	2-10D
hand stand push-ups	5	0	1	2	2-5

SPEED

Always warm-up thoroughly before practicing speed development exercises. Exercises marked with an asterisk (*) are exercises that are done for specific skills like punching, kicking or striking. If a set consists of ten repetitions, do ten repetitions for each kick, strike or punch you want to improve. Remember to work both sides. Start with a limited number of core skills for speed training so the length of your workout does not become overwhelming.

Exercise	Reps	Beg.	Int.	Adv.	#
50 yard sprint	3	1	2	3	3-5
50 yard uphill run	3	1	2	3	3-6
25 yard bounding	3	1	2	3	3-4
initiation drill	5*	1	2	3	3-1
relax & focus drill	5*	1	2	3	3-2
speed drill with target	10*	0	2	4	3-7
bicycle tube	10*	0	1	2	3-10
obstacle jump	10	2	3	5	3-8
whistle drill					
side to side	30 sec. 2	3	5		3-3
front to back	30 sec. 2	3	5		3-3B

FLEXIBILITY

Many of the flexibility exercises listed below do not increase in number as you progress. The nature of flexibility is such that quantity is not as important as quality. As you progress to the intermediate and advanced levels, the range of motion and correctness of your stretches should improve, leading to increased flexibility. Concentrate on stretching father with every workout.

Passive stretches, those do not require movement, are indicated with an asterisk (*) and should be held for about ten seconds per repetition. Remember to work both sides equally.

Exercise	Reps	Beg.	Int.	Adv.	#
neck rotation	10	1	1	1	8-1
large arm circles	10	1	1	1	8-2
small arm circles	10	1	2	3	8-2B
criss cross	10	1	1	1	8-21
press/press/fling	10	1	1	1	8-3
half windmill	10	1	1	1	8-4
up/back/over	10	1	1	1	8-22
arm raises	10	1	2	3	8-5
shoulder stretch	3*	1	1	1	8-6
rear arm stretch	3*	1	1	1	8-7
finger press	10	1	1	1	8-11
wrist flex	10	1	1	1	8-10

Exercise	Reps	Beg.	Int.	Adv.	#
inside forearm	10	1	1	1	8-8
outside forearm	10	1	1	1	8-9
trunk twist	10	1	2	3	8-12
trunk twist w/partner	5	1	2	3	8-24
trunk bend	10	1	1	1	8-13
hip rotation	5	1	1	1	8-25
knee rotation	5	1	1	1	8-26
toe touch	3*	1	1	1	8-27
groin stretch	3	1	2	3	8-28
knee raise and twist	5	2	3	4	8-29A
side bends	3	1	1	1	8-18
back lift	5	1	1	1	8-23
ankle rotation	10	1	1	1	8-31
seated trunk twist	5*	1	1	1	8-16
back stretch	5*	1	1	1	8-19
back roll	10	1	1	1	8-20

Exercise	Reps	Beg.	Int.	Adv.	#
butterfly stretch	5*	1	1	1	8-31
leg extension	5*	1	1	1	8-33
hurdler stretch	5*	1	1	1	8-35
knee pull	5*	1	1	1	8-32
double quadriceps	5*	0	1	1	8-34
saddle stretch	3*	1	2	3	8-37
side split	3*	0	1	2	8-36
center split	3*	0	1	2	8-36B
seated toe touch	5*	1	2	3	8-38
chest opening	5	1	2	3	8-14
lying trunk twist	5	1	2	3	8-17

MENTAL TRAINING

In mental training, as in flexibility, quality is the key. Try to improve your success rate and intensity for each exercise as you advance. Drills marked with an asterisk (*) are skill specific and should be done for each skill you want to improve. For example, bar practice has ten repetitions per set. This means ten repetitions of front kick, ten repetitions of side kick, ten repetitions of back kick, etc. Again, it is best to start with a few core skills for these drills. Remember to work both sides equally.

Exercise	Reps	Beg.	Int.	Adv.	#
jumping spin	8	1	2	2	4-1
standing spin & walk	1	1	2	3	4-2
bar practice	10*	1	2	3	10-3
hanging target	10*	1	2	3	10-6
speed bag	30 sec.	2	4	6	11-5
double end bag	30 sec.	2	4	6	11-6
focus pads	30 sec.	2	4	6	10-5
reaction drill	2 min.	0	2	4	11-3
target response	30 sec.	2	4	6	4-9
broken rhythm drill	1 min.	0	3	5	11-2
night tag	1 min.	1	2	3	4-10

Exercise	Reps	Beg.	Int.	Adv.	#
chalk sparring	1 min.	2	3	4	4-11
fast point sparring	1 min.	0	2	3	10-1
form with eyes closed	1*	2	3	4	4-5
dynamic tension	5*	1	2	3	10-2
visualization	1 min.	1	2	3	11-1

GLOSSARY

Aerobic energy - energy produced in the presence of oxygen

Anaerobic energy - energy produced using phosphates and stored glycogen without oxygen

Ballistic stretch - stretching muscles by bobbing, bouncing or other movements

Cardiovascular - pertaining to the heart and blood vessels

Center of gravity - the intersection of the lines of gravity for the vertical and horizontal orientations of the body. Indicates the point at which gravity acts regardless of the body's orientation relative to the ground.

Circuit training - periods of aerobic exercise interspersed with exercises to improve muscular strength and endurance.

Double ended bag - air filled ball with elastic tethers that attach to the floor and ceiling that is used for striking and kicking. Improves accuracy and timing.

Equilibrium - balance

Fascia - a fibrous sheath that surrounds and separates many muscles

Fast twitch muscle fiber - muscle tissue best suited to short, explosive activity

Focus glove - foam filled, leather covered mitt worn on the hand that is used for striking and kicking. Improves accuracy, speed and power.

Hand target - hand held foam paddle used for kicking and striking. Improves accuracy and speed.

Heavy bag - canvas or leather bag filled with sand, saw dust, rags or water that is used for kicking and striking. Improves power and endurance.

Interval training - short, intense bursts of exercise punctuated by periods of active rest

Isometric contraction - contraction in which one muscle lengthens and its opposing muscle is prevented from contracting

Isotonic contraction - contraction in which one muscle lengthens and its opposing muscle contracts

Ligament - tissue that binds bones or other internal structures

Motor unit - group of muscle fibers that work in concert

Myotatic reflex - also known as "stretch reflex" Reflex that responds to muscle lengthening by attempting to shorten the elongated muscle.

Repetition - completion of one exercise

Righting reflex - reflex that senses and controls upright posture

Slow twitch muscle fiber - muscle tissue best suited to low tension, endurance activities

Smooth muscle - muscles that perform involuntary functions.

Speed bag - teardrop shaped, leather ball filled with air and suspended from a circular platform that is used for striking. Improves timing, coordination and accuracy.

Striated muscle - muscles that perform voluntary functions.

Tendon - firm, inelastic cord that attaches muscle to bone

Vestibular apparatus - sensory organ of the inner ear whose primary function is to maintain balance.

Index

A

accuracy   205, 218
aerobic
  conditioning   195
  endurance   194-195
  energy   193-194
agility   91, 131
anaerobic
  endurance   195-196
  energy   194-195

B

balance   13-14, 91, 107, 131
  dynamic   107, 110
  static   107
breath control   27, 243

C

carbohydrates   237, 240
center of gravity   109-110, 111
circuit training   196
combination movements   106
coordination   91, 131

D

deconditioning   12, 28
detection   76
discrimination   76
dynamic balance   107
dynamic power   21
dynamic stretching   149

E

endurance   193
  and diet   240
  cardiovascular   193
  mental   227, 228
  muscular   193, 194-195, 196
execution speed   56, 59
explosive power   21

F

fascia   147
fast twitch fibers   23
fats   236-237
fitness
  benefits   10
  performance   10
flexibility   147

G

gravity   109-110
  center of   109-110, 111

I

identification   76
individuality   13
interval training   195-196
isometric   25
isotonic   24-25

J

joint pain   28, 150

L

Load   27

M

mental endurance   227, 228
mental strength   227-228
minerals   238
muscle fibers
  fast twitch   22-23
  slow twitch   22-23
muscle spindles   205-206
myotatic reflex   147, 148-149

N

nonspecific warm-up   14-15

nutrition   235

O

overload   12
overuse injuries   245

P

pain
   joint   28
passive warm-ups   14
perception   75, 131, 218
perception speed   55, 58
power
   dynamic   21
   explosive   21
   static   21
progression   27
protection gear   243
protein   236

R

range of motion   147, 148
reaction speed   56, 58
recognition   76
recovery speed   56, 60
repetitions   25-26, 27
reversibility   12
righting reflex   108-110

S

sets   27
slow twitch fibers   22
sparring   106, 132
specific warm-up   15
specificity   11-12
speed   55-56, 91, 131, 217, 218
   execution   56, 59
   perception   55, 58
   reaction   56, 58-59
   recovery   56, 60
static balance   107
static power   21
static stretching   149

strength   131
stretching
   ballistic   149
   dynamic   149
   static   149

T

timing   91, 217

V

vestibular apparatus   108-109
visualization   93
vitamins   238

W

warm-up
   effects of   14
   function of   13
   how to   27, 242
   non-specific   14-15
   passive   14
   specific   15
   types of   14-17
water   238-239

Other books available from Turtle Press:

Teaching: The Way of the Master
Combat Strategy
The Art of Harmony
Rape Awareness and Prevention
Advanced Teaching Report
Taekwondo Kyorugi: Olympic Style Sparring
Launching a Martial Arts School
Hosting a Martial Arts Tournament

For more information:
Turtle Press
PO Box 290206
Wethersfield CT 06129-0206
Phone: 1-800-77-TURTLE